The African American Christian Family: Building Lasting Relationships

Eddie B. Lane

Publisher

Black Family Press
1810 Park Row
Dallas, Texas 75215
(214) 428-3761

Published in the United States of America

Cover Design: Fame Publishing Inc.

TABLE OF CONTENTS

PART 1

THE INSTITUTION OF MARRIAGE

PART 2

THE CHRISTIAN HOME

PART 3

FAMILY COMMUNICATION

PART 4

CONFLICT MANAGEMENT

PART 5

SEX EDUCATION

PART 6

EQUIPPING FOR THE STRUGGLE

DEDICATION

The story is told of a preacher who accidently encountered a neatly wrapped box on the top shelf of the closet in his master bedroom. He inquired of his wife what was in that box. She replied that its contents were of no great significance, and she would appreciate it if he would simply forget that he ever saw the box and go on his way.

Shortly afterwards his wife went shopping. His curiosity got the best of him and he removed the box from the shelf. Much to his surprise, inside the box were three eggs and two thousand dollars. He closed the box and put it back on the shelf.

When his wife returned from the store, the preacher asked her again about the contents of the box. "Well," the wife replied, "as you know I have been with you in the ministry for some thirty-two years now. I have listened to almost all of your sermons and whenever you delivered a bad sermon, I put an egg in that box." The preacher was pleased that in thirty-two years she only had three eggs in the box, but was still puzzled about the two thousand dollars. She explained, "Each time I got a dozen eggs in the box, I sold them."

On July 4, 1995 Betty and I celebrated thirty years of Christian ministry. Had she done what this preacher's wife did, we would be quite wealthy today. Betty was 19 years old when I asked her to marry me. When she was twenty, we were married in the recreation center of the projects in South Dallas. Since that wonderful day we have never been separated.

This book is dedicated to my wife Betty Jo Washington Lane. Many do not have the opportunity to meet her because she is not in the public's eye. The contents of this book, however, are the direct result of her influence on my life and the ministry. I was blessed of God to marry a wonderful, strong African American woman.

Thanks Betty for helping me through fifteen years of Bible school, college and seminary. Thanks for caring for me during my twenty-five year struggle with colitis. Thanks for being a real mother to our children. Thanks for staying with me through the many years of hard times and real sacrifice.

There is an old adage that says, "behind every good man there is a strong woman." That may be true. I lay no claim to being a good man; but whatever I am, I must say that my wife has not been behind me; she has always been beside me as my friend, companion, lover, and number one struggling-buddy. God's greatest gift to me is my wife. No other person could be so deserving as my lovely wife, Betty.

ACKNOWLEDGEMENTS

It was my privilege to be born the fourth child of John and Cleo Lane. Today both my parents are with the Lord. I am but a small testimony to the kind of parents they were to their children.

Thank you Mom and Dad for the multitude of sacrifices you made to "grow" children who had a sense of family. I do not wish to boast but I think you did a good job.

I want to acknowledge many friends who have helped me think and rethink my ideas about marriage and family life. Some worked with the organization and layout; some edited and typed the manuscripts; while others provided immeasurable resources. Although the list is much too long to mention, some must be noted. They are: Lafayette E. Holland, Mary A. Wallace, Don and Charlotte Test, Lin Williams, Mary H. Crossland, and Billie Stafford.

I am deeply indebted to Bibleway Bible Church and all the members who have supported me in various ways over the years . . . giving me the liberty to grow and develop a number of ministries within and outside the church.

Like many people of my generation, I grew up in the South in a home in which love was assumed and people stayed together often because that was the thing to do in those days. My parents were like other parents of that era. They worked hard on the farm, and gave their four children the best they could afford.

My parents were limited in many ways; but in spite of their limitations in the social and oppressive context of East Carrol Parish in Lake Providence, Louisiana, my dad taught me the meaning of integrity and hard work. Even though he was functionally illiterate himself, he gave me a thirst for knowledge. My dad taught me how to value the best things in life. He equipped me with discernment and taught me never to be afraid of anybody no matter their color. He taught me to stand up for what I thought was right. He taught me the value of the family.

My dear mother taught me sensitivity and compassion. She taught me the meaning of giving of one's self for the good of others. She taught me love and tenderness. As the youngest of four children, I was always special in the eyes of my mother. To her I was the brightest, the smartest, and above all—I was her baby. My mother was a model of compassion and forgiveness. she never tired of helping others and as a result, every hungry person in the community knew that they always had a place at her table.

It is out of this background that I have evolved into the man I am today. You will discover in this book that I am a man of my African American context, committed to the resurrected Jesus Christ in service to His church.

The focus of this book is on the African American Christian family. Having said that, I realize that some

Christians are of the opinion that there is no difference in what the Bible says to African American families and what it says to other Christian families. To this I agree completely. However, I am of the opinion that the legacy of the Black family in North America and the contemporary social and economic context in which Black families exist in this country are very different from other ethnicities and cultures. The application of biblical principles and the resultant solution to family problems are very different from other groups.

This book is divided into six sections, written from the perspective of providing solutions to issues facing the African American family today. It is my hope and prayer that its contents will minister to you and your family.

PART 1

THE INSTITUTION OF MARRIAGE

CHAPTER 1

SEX AND SEXUALITY IN AMERICA

There are few things that have changed more in the past twenty years than has the role of sex and sexuality. Among the institutions that have been most profoundly affected in a negative way by this change is the family. The pursuit of sex and its pleasure has virtually destabilized the African American family and thereby created a major social crisis that must be faced by most families in North America. The most destabilizing factor in the family is that husbands and wives will divorce after many years of marriage to pursue a sexual relationship with someone else. This happens among the rich as well as among the poor. It happens among the saved and among the unsaved. It is as common among Whites as it is among African Americans. In the modern day American home, sex is in reality a stronger bond than strong character, economic security, or Christian commitment.

Recently a major television network aired a documentary on divorce among people in their sixties. The impact of a drastic change in sexual attitudes was the main topic discussed. Most of the men interviewed divorced their wives of many years and married younger women with little regard for the future welfare of their former wives. This report pointed out that the new sexual practice gives men more options than it does women. Older men often, for a variety of reasons, pursue and attract younger women;

older women usually do not have or want this option.

These were husbands and wives who had made their living and raised their families. At sixty, however, they decided that their need for sexual pleasure was more important than their marriage commitment. They divorced and married someone else for the pleasure of sex and the excitement of sexuality.

As a pastor I see a number of women in their fifties and sixties in the church who are caught in the fallout of the new sexual attitude of their mates. They are struggling with disappointment and bitterness due to the infidelity of their husbands.

In the environment of contemporary sexual attitude, homosexuality is now considered a viable option. Men burn in their lustful attraction to men; women also vie for their own gender. At the heart of these "out-of-the-closet" relationships is the pursuit of physical gratification under the guise of a "right" to sexual freedom. It should be noted that the AIDS virus is spreading fast among African American women. This can be traced to the new sexual practices of men which are not stemmed by fear of this deadly virus. It means that a growing number of men are bisexual in their sexual preferences.

Considering the role of sex and sexuality in relationships, we should note that both have evolved to a point where there are no moral, social or religious boundaries— no limitations—no right and wrong. In the contemporary sexual environment, one does what one feels, when one feels it, with whomever one wishes. Such attitudes have essentially moved the marriage benchmark for commitment and longevity into the realm of the relative. In a real sense it can be said today that a marriage is only as secure as the couple's satisfaction with their sex life, in spite of everything else they might share together. There are fewer people, even in the church, who can honestly say that they believe that sex outside of marriage is wrong. They might believe it to be unsafe or maybe even unwise, but hardly wrong, especially if the two people love one another but are simply not married.

Among the married, the benchmark has also been moved by the so-called sexual revolution so that sex outside of marriage with discretion is considered to be acceptable as long as the couple understands one another.

This being the case, such words as adultery and fornication have become irrelevant, even in the church.

Bill and Mary, two successful professionals, had been married for more than twenty years. They had several children and a strong religious and social life. Then Bill became attracted to his wife's best friend. The relationship between Bill and his wife's friend continued for several years. During this time Bill sought to convince his wife that such a relationship was no big deal as long as he faithfully met all of her needs. Bill's idea was to have both a wife and a mistress who were friends and were both committed to meeting his needs. Fortunately, Bill's wife had a sense of right and wrong that would not allow her to accept this adulterous arrangement.

The Bible is not silent on the role of sex and sexuality in marriage. Genesis 2:24-25 sets forth the "one flesh" concept. From the very beginning of human kind, the "one flesh" concept was God's way of binding men and women in a lifetime commitment to one another. This bonding exists not only among humans, but also among some species in the animal kingdom. I began to observe this bonding phenomenon at the funeral of spouses. The spouse of the deceased grieved as though a very vital part of his/her being had been lost, was irreplaceable and life would not be the same without it.

William and Billie had been married for more than sixty years when William succumbed to illness and old age and eventually died. During the period of William's sickness, I observed Billie's attentiveness to his every need. She hardly gave the nurses an opportunity to do anything for him. She constantly talked to him when he became comatose. Even in that state, William and Billie were communicating with one another.

At William's funeral, Billie stared at his body and said, "William, William I miss you so much." A few months after William's funeral, Billie died. Before she died she communicated to her children that she had no reason to continue living because the one she loved most had moved to heaven and that was where she wanted to be. It was this experience that set me thinking about the concept of bonding in marriage.

In bonding, sex is the consummation of the physical and emotional essence in a seven-step process. It begins with the "me-to-you" phase which may be brought on by physical attraction or a variety of other shared attractions. This is followed by the following stages: eye-to-eye, hand-to-hand, hand-to-body, lip-to-lip, hand-to-genitals, and finally, genitals-to-genitals bonding. The tragic thing about contemporary attitude towards sex is that people are "fast forwarding" and initiating genitals-to-genitals contact with a mere "pause" at the six preceding steps.

It is the contention of those who study sex and sexuality that sex holds a higher priority in America than it does in any other place in the world. America has the sexually transmitted disease record that goes with this distinction. In the American media, there are more products sold with sexual overtones than there are without sexual overtones. Primetime television is filled with sexually explicit implications and suggestions. It could be concluded that in the mind of most Americans, sex is considered to be more valuable than any other human commodity.

It is said that when great ancient Egyptian pharaohs died they embalmed their bodies using a process that caused mummification. This was done to provide a dwelling place for their karma. In preparation for burial the stomach, intestines, and other organs were removed and preserved in separate vessels. The heart was left in the body, while the brain (a useless organ) was thrown away.

The social environment today is not unlike that of the ancient Egyptians in terms of how we tend to view our brains. Our youth are given the idea that there is no recognized use for the brain. It is clearly communicated to them that the most valuable assets one can have are a great body and great sex. Need one wonder why they give little thought to cooking their brains with drugs.

In spite of society's obsession with sex, the Christians' focus must be on and remain on the individual. It must be understood that sex is perhaps one of our strongest drives. However, this does not at all mean this desire cannot be controlled. As important as sex is, it is necessary for Christians to view their mates as more than a sex partner. To move in the direction of restoring the structure of the marriage and putting sex in its proper perspective, it will be necessary for the Christian to move away from a focus on the physical and move towards a focus that is inclusive of the whole person, that is, body, soul and spirit.

In a recent Bible study, I was teaching 1 Corinthians chapter seven when I called attention to verse 5 which says, "Stop depriving one another, except by agreement for a time that you may devote yourselves to prayer, and come together again lest Satan tempt you because of your lack of self control" (NASB). I made the point that it is wise for Christians to always keep their sex life before the Lord in prayer less they neglect it and give the devil an opportunity to exploit their unfulfilled sexual desires.

Eric and Shelia had been married for more than twenty years when Eric began to experience difficulty in responding to Shelia's aggressive sexual desires. Eric's inability was both frightening and humiliating. Like most African American men, Eric decided not to talk about his problem, choosing rather to avoid the issue by withdrawing from his wife under guise of being busy and under serious pressure from his job.

When Shelia finally confronted Eric about his increasing lack of interest in sex he responded by saying that sex was not very important in marriage and in his opinion far too much emphasis was given to the role of sex in marriage. With this said, Eric resumed his role as the overburdened and too busy husband. However, the lack of sexual activity combined with Eric's silence and withdrawals, soon began to create serious frustration and irritation in both Eric and Shelia toward each other.

In time, when Shelia decided that she would no longer tolerate Eric's evasive attitude and behavior toward her, they both decided to get counseling. In the first session it was evident that this couple had become negligent in their responses to each other as it pertained to their respective sexual needs.

Like so many African American men, sexual impotence was for Eric a cause for shame and embarrassment. He felt he was losing his manhood, which for an African American man was a fate worse than death. The counselor suggested to Eric that he consult a physician and that they both make their sex life a matter of consistent prayer before the Lord.

It had been twelve years since I married Sue and Malcolm when it became evident that they were having serious marital problems. Malcolm was a good man who worked hard but found it most difficult to come home after work, choosing rather to spend time hanging out with the boys.

While Malcolm hung out in the streets, Sue found her security by hanging out with the women in the church. I noticed that Sue was increasingly given to a new form of spiritual excitement and expression that was inconsistent with her temperament in years past.

In counseling Malcolm raised the issue of what the Bible said about a wife's responsibility to her husband in the area of sex. After reminding both of them of what the Bible taught in this area Malcolm pointedly said, "Is it right for a wife to schedule the day and time she will be available to her husband for sex?" The problem was a failure on the part of Sue to put the same level of priority on their sex life as did her husband. In this case Satan was exploiting the negligence by creating conflict and frustration in both Malcolm and Sue.

CHAPTER 2

MARRIAGE:
A DIVINE INSTITUTION

In discussing the issue of divorce with the Pharisees in Matthew 19, it is essential to note that the Pharisees started this discussion with Jesus concerning their contemporary religiously sanctioned view of divorce and remarriage as the accepted social standard of that day. Their view of divorce and remarriage allowed a man to divorce his wife for any reason and at his discretion, marry someone else.

Note their question in Matthew 19:3: "Is it lawful for a man to divorce his wife for any cause at all?" Their question revealed their motive which was twofold. First, they wanted approval of what they were already doing and second, they wanted to discredit Jesus in the eyes of the people—if He dared to disagree with what Moses had taught about divorce and remarriage. You see, in the minds of the Pharisees, they had truly ambushed Jesus leaving Him with only two options. He could either affirm what they were practicing, which was sentencing mostly older women to a life of abuse and abandonment, or He could disagree with Moses and discredit Himself in the eyes of the Jewish religious community.

We must also call attention to the disciples' response to the Lord's discussion of the subject of divorce and remarriage with the Pharisees. Having heard the discussion, the disciples said to Jesus, "If the relationship of a man with his wife is like you have just said, it's better for a man not to marry." Jesus did not disagree with the disciples' conclusion. In view of the fact that there were no exits in marriage, it is better not to marry. Jesus also said that a life of celibacy is not a possibility for everybody. For those who have a relationship with God, being a single adult means being a celibate adult.

In the context of the religious community of that day, there were three different views on divorce. One view was that a marriage was to last as long as the man wanted it to last. Whenever he got tired of a wife, he could simply give her a certificate of divorce for any reason and send her away. Having divorced his wife, the man could go on to the next woman and marry her. In this context, divorce was a man's thing; there was no option for the woman. The second view held that once married it was not possible to get out of that marriage for any reason. In view of the permanency of marriage, a third view emerged, namely, a man could either marry and remain married no matter what or he could remain single.

Now these three concepts differ in content, but they share or raise the same question, what is a person to do if the marriage proves to be a bad connection for some reason? The Pharisees' response to a marriage gone bad was to get out of it. The disciples' response was to avoid the possibility of a bad one by remaining single.

We must arrive at the solution of the problem of divorce and remarriage. Jesus does not start with the contemporary view of the Pharisees, which they based on the teaching of Moses. He also did not begin with the emotional response of His disciples which they based on common sense. To resolve the problem of divorce, Jesus took the discussion back to the beginning of time as we know it. He started His discussion about marriage and divorce back in the garden of Eden with the first marriage that ever was, the marriage between Adam and Eve. In order to get a biblical perspective, Jesus went back to God's ideal rather than starting with man's contemporary view of marriage.

Our Lord's reply to the Pharisees' question about the validity of divorce and remarriage was succinct. "Have you not read that He who created them from the beginning made them male and female and said for this cause a man shall leave his father and his mother and shall cleave to his wife and the two shall be one flesh?"

It is interesting to note that our Lord goes back to the beginning of the human race to deal with the subject of divorce and remarriage. By going back to the beginning of the human race to answer the Pharisees' question, He removes the issue out of the context of the contemporary religious teaching which they were practicing and elevates the institution of marriage and the principles that govern it above the teachings of Moses.

The point that Jesus is making about the institution of marriage is that the creation of man, woman and marriage are all divine acts. Neither of these three divine acts could have been accomplished by man. It is interesting to note, that in every culture regardless of the religion, and even in atheistic countries, there is some concept of marriage and in most instances there is also some concept of divorce. It could well be concluded that the universal practice of marriage and family is evidence of the fact that it is a divine idea. The only people who have a history that includes a time in which marriage and family was officially denied them is the African American under slavery.

During that "peculiar institution," the work of abolitionists exceeded just getting them out of the slave states. Once they were free, the former slaves had to be taught a sense of family. The same was true in the post-emancipation era; the freed slaves had to be taught a sense of family. In order to have any sense of humanity and basic human dignity, a person must have a sense of family. Being human and being family are essential to being people. The African American church was the primary teaching agent in this historical context.

The subject of divorce is tied to the concept of marriage. Thus to deal with the issue of divorce, it is necessary to begin with the concept of marriage as God instituted it between Adam and Eve in the garden of Eden. Marriage is not an idea or concept that man stumbled upon in time after he crawled up out of some primordial swamp through the process of evolution. Even the so-called "primitive man" had some concept of marriage and family. Marriage is as old as man. Marriage was created by God at the same time that He created man. There has never been a time in the history of the existence of man that marriage and family were not a part of mankind's social mores. It would seem possible, therefore, to conclude that marriage and family are a necessary part of what it means to be a human being as opposed to some lesser animal. Yes, there is a thing called bonding for life among some animals and birds; but there is no concept of marriage and family among these creatures.

Today in North America, approximately 51 percent of all African American children are born out of wedlock. More than a few of these children are born to women who are socially classified as the underclass. This means that such children most often grow into adult men and women with no sense of family. To the extent that a sense of humanity and human dignity are tied to one's sense of family, to that extent we may be growing adults who have little sense of their own humanity and little sense of human dignity. A primary characteristic of such people is that they are given to acting out what they feel at the moment and getting what they want without consideration of the consequences.

God did not leave man at the mercy of his desires as are the lesser animals that He created. When God created man and woman, he also created the context within which all of their desires and goals were to be nurtured and expressed.

At the very outset of the marriage relationship, God establishes the principle that the marriage relationship between a man and his wife is their primary relationship. There is no other relationship that either the man or the woman has that is to exceed their marriage relationship. Even the parent-child relationship is to be subordinate to it. Marriage is divinely arranged to be the single mandated lifelong relationship. All other relationships are optional in terms of their duration.

At the very beginning, it is to be noted that God's principles regarding marriage evolves around the man and not the woman. I think this is more than a cultural thing since race and culture were not relevant in the context of the marriage between Adam and Eve. They were the only race and culture in the whole world. The principles regarding marriage were entrusted to the man because man was and is the crown of God's creation. God entrusted the future of the institution of marriage to the man.

To the man God said, "Leave your father and your mother and cleave to your wife." This is a principle that was spoken to Adam and Eve but had nothing to do with their marriage because Adam and Eve had neither mother nor father. It was meant for future generations.

The man who takes a wife is to leave his parents and cleave to his wife. For the son this is an emotional separation and the beginning of a new area of emotional growth. This means that the marriage between this man and woman takes priority over the relationship they have with their parents. The creation of marriage at the same time that man and woman were created teaches us that from God's perspective, an adult male can live without parents. Those without the gift of celibacy, however, need a wife. God did not create parents for Adam; he did create for him a wife.

In Genesis 2 God makes the observation that it is not good for man to be alone, and He resolved to create for man a helper suitable for him. Before God created a corresponding helper for Adam, He sensitized Adam to the fact that he was alone and needed a helper suitable for him. Having made Adam aware of his need for a wife, God created Eve and gave her to Adam. In responding to Adam's need for female companionship, God gave him one woman who was to be his wife for the rest of his life. God did not give him two or more women, just one. This one was his wife. I take it, therefore, that in the mind of God, one woman is sufficient for any man for his whole life. In the first marriage there was no provision made for separation and or divorce.

In pointed fact: it is God not society that makes a marriage. The commitment to marriage is the kind of commitment that includes God as a part of that which binds a man to his wife. Jesus Christ said, "What therefore God has joined together, let no man separate" (Mark 10:9). This statement takes the option of divorce out of the hands of everybody on this earth, including the courts.

Marriage is a sacred institution. It was established by God. To tamper with marriage is to tamper with the sacred. God hates divorce. "Let marriage be held in honor by all, and let the marriage bed be undefiled" (Heb. 13:4).

CHAPTER 3

SEXUAL INTERCOURSE: CONSUMMATION OF THE MARRIAGE VOWS

At the very beginning of the marriage and family life of man and woman, God introduced the "one-flesh" concept in Genesis 2:24-25. We see it again in Mark 10:6-8 and in Matthew 19:5-6. In the text the concept of one flesh is brought forth in the discussion of divorce in the New Testament (Matt.19).

We know the one flesh concept is related to sex because in the Genesis text it is said that the man and the woman were both naked and were not ashamed. The "one-flesh" concept is specifically related to sex in 1 Corinthians 6:16, "Or do you not know that the one who joins himself to a harlot is one body with her?" For He says, 'the two will become one flesh.' " It has reference to sexual intercourse between a man and a woman.

The question remains, how is the one flesh concept related to marriage? In the Old Testament it is evident that God established sexual intercourse as the means by which marriage was consummated. In Deuteronomy 22:13-30 the law of God as given by Moses is reviewed as it pertains to sexual activity among the people of God. In every instance where a man had sex with a woman, she either became his wife, or both of them were stoned to death for committing adultery if either of them were married or engaged. To have sex with a woman who was not an engaged virgin was to get for oneself a wife that could never be divorced. To have sex with a woman who was engaged was to get for oneself the penalty of death by stoning. For a woman to have sex by choice outside of marriage was to get for herself the penalty of death by stoning. To violate God's moral code in any unacceptable form would mean death.

Sexual intercourse was established by God from the very beginning of human history as that which consummates a marriage. It is still true today that sexual intercourse is the means by which marriage is consummated. "Let the marriage bed be undefiled; fornicators and adulterers God will judge" (Heb. 13:4).

Man is the crown of God's creation. God said that it was not good for man to be alone. Thus God sensitized man to his need to have a wife who would be his corresponding helper. God made for Adam an Eve and gave her to him as his wife. So from the very beginning, God created man and then he created a woman, Eve, to be his wife. The marriage between Adam and Eve was consummated by sex. We have man, woman and sex bound together for life at the very beginning of humankind on this earth. In other words, we have a family. God's ideal social state for humankind, with few exceptions, is marriage and family. The act that consummates the marriage is sex.

In the creation narrative in Genesis 1 and 2, it is interesting that Adam was not aware that he was alone and that this state was not good for him. The fact that he was not cognizant of his state did not diminish the fact that he was alone and needed an Eve. It is at this point that the relationship between a man and woman in our day is determined in terms of the quality of their relationship in general and as husband and wife in particular. How men and women relate to one another is based entirely upon each one's perception of why they need the other.

Until Adam came to grips with the fact that he was created as one part of a two part single unit and in his present situation he was alone and this situation was not good for him, there was no possibility of him ever relating to Eve as his corresponding helper.

One of the major problems in contemporary marriage relationships is the fact that young men are reveling in their independence and newly discovered intellectual accomplishments. They tend to be woefully out of touch with their emotions and are therefore unable to relate to their need for a corresponding helper. Perhaps the best description of the modern day man is that he is alone and that is not good for him. Man having divested himself of all that is divine and spiritual has created for himself a new religion of intellectualism and surrounded himself with things and the power to satisfy his need to rule. In this context, man has little need for a woman who is his corresponding helper. His need for a woman is almost exclusively physical, relating only to his biology and his desire to reproduce himself.

We must be careful not to exclude women from the modern day dilemma of the family. If we are to believe Genesis 2:18-25, then we must embrace the idea that God created women in response to Adam's need for a corresponding helper. God did not create Eve to compete with Adam, but to be his corresponding helper. Eve was in every way Adam's equal, yet she was God's gift to him. Adam was not created for Eve but Eve was created for Adam. A major part of the marriage problem today is women are no longer content with the idea that they were created as man's corresponding helper. Women have always been equal to men from God's perspective so that equality with man is not a biblical issue. The biblically specified difference between men and women is and has always been a difference of roles and functions. It has never been a matter of equality. The contemporary woman does not see herself as a dependent creature as it pertains to her relationship with men in general and a husband in particular. She, like the man, is to be found reveling in her accomplishments surrounded by her freedom and things.

In the church as in the world, sex and marriage have become something less than sacred. Marriage is no longer viewed as a union for life. Sex is no longer that which consummates a marriage; it is more a badge of liberation. Today, even in the church, virginity for both male and female is a state of which one is ashamed.

In premarital counseling, serious work must be done to establish God's ideal of marriage in the minds and hearts of the couple. It cannot be assumed that the couple has convictions about marriage that are consistent with the biblical idea.

I have found that more than a few of the couples that I counseled have grown up without the presence of their own mother and father in the same household. Therefore more than a few of these young men are spiritually, emotionally and socially unprepared to be the head of a wife. They have no model of the nuclear family . . . no idea of what it means to lead in love.

It is also evident that more than a few couples are bringing to the marriage altar a myriad of sexual experiences that will forever be a part of their sexual attitude. The sexual experiences are nothing less than ghosts in the bedroom of the couple that can contribute to a variety of problems that must be dealt with. When all is said and done, the biblical idea of moral purity is still the best idea.

CHAPTER 4

THE HARD HEART:
THE ROOT OF
MARITAL PROBLEMS

I t is no secret that among Christians there are almost
as many divorces today as there are marriages. The sad
truth is that marriage vows actually should read until
death or divorce do we part, whichever comes first. About
half the parents who see their children marry today will
witness their divorce. This raises the question, what happened to God's ideal? In other words, if God is against divorce, why is it that it has become such a common thing?

In Matthew 19, the Pharisees questioned Jesus regarding divorce. They asked, "If it is not right to divorce your
wife, then why did Moses permit the giving of a certificate
of divorce to a wife that one no longer wanted?" This question raised the issue as to whether what Moses had permitted regarding divorce superseded what God had already
said at the beginning in Genesis 2? In answering this question, Jesus said no and that what Moses did had no effect
on what God established in the beginning regarding marriage and divorce. He took the discussion back to the beginning to show that God had not altered what He said in
the beginning: marriage is for life.

The fall of man did not change God's absolutes concerning the permanence of marriage. Marriage was established to be a relationship between one man and one

woman for life before the fall and it remained after the fall. The entry of total depravity into the heart of man did not move God's ideal for marriage beyond the reach of man. However, the entry of sin into the human experience did so alter the human heart of man that his attitude towards marriage, as God had designed it, began to change. A desire developed in the heart of man to be free from the bond of marriage as God had designed it.

In Matthew 19 that attitude is described as hardheartedness. In other words, sin tampered with the heart of man and caused him to become unwilling to practice such virtues as patience, understanding, and forgiveness. Thus, the conflicts that disturb the unity of marriage had no means by which they could be resolved. In view of this kind of attitude, Moses permitted the men to give the women they no longer wanted a certificate of divorce and send them away. However, this was not intended to establish divorce as an alternative to living in a problematic marriage. Divorce is the fruit of ungodly attitudes in godly people and should be treated that way.

Henry and Salome had been married for almost seven years when things began to fall apart. In their marriage Henry had always been something less than responsible in managing their finances. He willingly stood in the shadows of his wife when it came to earning money, but he freely spent what she earned. After nearly seven years, Salome had decided that she would no longer carry her husband and the children. When asked why she had married Henry, she responded, "I knew that Henry had problems when we married; but since we both were saved, I thought we could work them out. I was wrong and I have had enough." In the years of their marriage Henry proved himself to be unforgiving, impatient and negligent. In time the same unChristian attitudes were manifested in his wife. In most instances divorce is a matter of the heart.

The permission to give an unwanted wife a certificate of divorce was an act of mercy on God's part toward women through Moses. During that epoch when a man no longer wanted a woman, he simply put her out, refusing to provide for her any longer. For many women, this meant starving to death since the most common reason for putting a wife out was age. She was too old for employment and not available for suitors. To put an end to this kind of abuse of women, Moses instructed the men to give the un-wanted wife a certificate of divorce and send her away. By so doing, she could possibly marry someone else. I must hasten to point out two things at this juncture. This action by Moses was not God's plan from the beginning. Hard-heartedness was not to characterize Jesus' disciples who were listening to this discussion along with the Pharisees.

I have sought to make the point that in many in-stances divorce is the result of hard-heartedness in which the will to forgive is absent. The heart willing to forgive offenses and open the door to reconciliation between the offender and the offended, is a tender heart. Reconcilia-tion in the spiritual context between God and man is a theological term declaring restoration of communion be-tween God and man. In its essence reconciliation points backward to a previous relationship of union and com-munication between God and man that was broken by man's offense against God. Reconciliation also affirms a resolution of the offense that severed the tie between God and man by appeasing the wrath of God against man

In order to appease God's wrath and bring about rec-onciliation, it was necessary for God to provide a way by which the offense that severed the relationship with man could be propitiated. Jesus Christ was God's provision. He settled the offense between God and man by paying the penalty for man's sin against God with His own blood and thereby propitiating (i.e., satisfying) God's wrath.

This pattern of reconciliation provides us with a pat-tern for reconciliation between the offended and the of-fender in the context of marriage. There are at least three factors involved in the biblical pattern of reconciliation:

1. There must be a recognized need for reconcilia-tion. This involves an acknowledgement of a past relationship that was broken by an offense.
2. One of the parties must take the initiative in es-tablishing a way of propitiating the offense. The provision must be adequate, just, and efficacious for both parties.
3. Both the offender and the offended must be willing to deal in accord with the terms of the established pattern for reconciliation.

The goal of forgiveness and reconciliation is the reso-lution of the offense that occurred in the relationship. To resolve the offense the offender must repent of the offense. On the part of the offended, resolution of the offense means being willing to forgive both offense and offender.

Matthew 18:21-27 says, "Then Peter came and said to Him, 'Lord, how often shall my brother sin against me and I forgive him? Up to seven times?' Jesus said to him, 'I do not say to you, up to seven times, but up to seventy times seven. For this reason the kingdom of heaven may be compared to a certain king who wished to settle accounts with his slaves. And when he had begun to settle them, there was brought to him one who owed him ten thousand talents. But since he did not have the means to repay, his lord commanded him to be sold, along with his wife and children and all that he had, and repayment to be made. The slave therefore falling down, prostrated himself before him, saying, "Have patience with me, and I will repay you everything." And the lord of that slave felt compassion and released him and forgave him the debt.' "

In reconciliation the offense must be handled in such a way that the integrity of the offender is not compromised nor the offense rationalized. This must be done to prevent the offended from feeling exploited and the offender from carrying perpetual guilt, thus negating the fruits of reconciliation.

In reconciliation between God and man, God (the offended) initiated the process. He established the terms of reconciliation. It is important to note that the terms of reconciliation between God and man are designed to protect the integrity of both God and man. In reconciliation God had to be both just and the justifier and man had to perceive God's love and his (man's) own personal freedom. The terms provided that the sin debt had to be paid, which God did in Christ, and man had to repent. Similarly, in terms of reconciliation between people, the offender must truly repent of the evil done to the offended, and the offended must likewise be persuaded not to persist in charging the offender with the offense (see Matt. 18:25-35).

Reconciliation begins in a heart that is willing to forgive. However, forgiveness and reconciliation, must not be made to mean that the offender can persist in the offense. Such conduct most often produces a feeling of exploitation in the offended and guilt in the offender which most often leads to permanent separation and ultimately divorce.

CHAPTER 5

ADULTERY:
THE MARRIAGE DISSOLVER

T his final point takes us back to the original question stated in Matthew 19:3, "Is it lawful for a man to divorce his wife for any cause at all?" The answer to this question is found in Matthew 19:9. Here it is made clear that it is possible for a man/woman to divorce his/her mate and marry another person if their mate commits adultery. Let me state my personal conviction: infidelity and/or desertion by an unbeliever are the only grounds for divorce and remarriage among the people of God.

You will remember that I have argued that sexual intercourse is the means by which a marriage is consummated. I have sought to demonstrate this from the Book of Deuteronomy 22 and other passages. In Deuteronomy, it is said that a man who has sex with a single unengaged woman had for all practical purposes gotten for himself a wife for life. To have sex with a woman who was single, but engaged or married was to get for himself the penalty of death by stoning. A woman who was found to have been sexually active outside of marriage was put to death by stoning. From the very beginning sexual intercourse was established as the means by which marriage was consummated. To so consummate a marriage was to become one flesh. In marriage the one flesh concept through sexual union is the sacred bond of marriage.

As we consider the grounds for divorce and remarriage

as set forth by Jesus in Matthew 19, it is sexual intercourse with someone other than your mate that breaks the marriage bond and frees the innocent party to remarry another. In other words, that which consummates a marriage is sex between a man and his wife; likewise, that which breaks the marriage bond is sex when done with someone other than that mate. It is my contention that in such situations, the innocent party is the one who is free to remarry. The reason I say that the innocent person is free to marry again is because the guilty party in the Jewish community of that day would have been put to death as a means of purging sin from among the people of God.

In all of His teachings on this subject of divorce and remarriage, Jesus speaks only to the subject of immorality as that which destroys the marriage bond. He does not address the issue of how the courts treat a marriage. The sin that destroys a marriage is in the hearts of the married couple. Going to the courts for a legal verdict is only a subsequent result. A marriage that is disrupted for any reason, including infidelity, has as much possibility of being reconciled as the couple will allow. It depends on the tenderness of their hearts and the presence or absence of the will to forgive.

Having heard the Lord's discussion on and clarification of the issue of divorce and remarriage, the disciples concluded that it was better not to marry than to marry and never be able to dissolve it if it is not a good marriage. Jesus never said to the disciples that they had misunderstood what He said about the finality of marriage. He did say that the opinion to remain single is not an option for everyone. Some people lack the wherewithal to remain single and moral; for those people marriage is a must. However, to marry is to make a lifetime commitment.

The Bible teaches that marriage is to be held in honor by all and the marriage bed undefiled (Heb. 13:4). The reason marriage is to be held in honor by all Christians is because it is the first ordinance God instituted after He created man and woman. God Himself, personally gave away the first bride and then performed the first wedding. The text says God gave the woman Eve to Adam and they became one flesh.

God instituted marriage for at least three reasons and I think these are relevant today. First, God created marriage as the ideal context for rearing whole and healthy human beings (Gen. 1:27-28). In Genesis the propagation of the human race is set forth. God's command was to be fruitful and multiply. Second, God designed marriage as a preventative against immorality. First Corinthians 7:2 indicates that in order to avoid fornication every man should have his own mate. Third, marriage is designed to circumvent loneliness (Gen. 2:18-25).

Shannon and Monica were married about four years when they began to experience difficulty in their relationship. Shannon discovered that Monica was having an affair. His reaction to this was to become physically and verbally violent.

When Shannon came to see me, he had just put Monica out of the house after abusing her. In great detail Shannon explained to me how he felt about this situation. Finally he asked me if it was possible for him, as a Christian, to divorce his wife and possibly remarry. I told him it was my opinion that he had that option. Then, I added, divorce was not the only option he had. It is possible to manage and survive infidelity.

The marriage vows most often include this statement: "In taking the woman whom you hold by the right hand to be your lawful and wedded wife, I require you to promise to love and cherish her, to honor and sustain her in sickness and in health, in poverty and in wealth, in the bad that may darken your days, in the good that may light your way, and to be true to her in all things until death alone shall part you."

The very fabric of this marriage vow is commitment. In specific words it expresses the preeminence of fidelity and loyalty in marriage. In spite of the specificity of the language, infidelity in marriage is one of the primary causes of divorce. But there is an alternative to divorce even when there has been adultery.

In managing and surviving adultery it is important to begin with the idea that in most instances infidelity is not about love for another person, but rather a means of striking or rebelling against the mate. It is perhaps the most vicious form of emotional battering and social degrading of one's mate. It happens most often not as an act of love for the adulterous partner but rather it is an expression of anger at the mate.

In terms of managing infidelity it is important to note that moral convictions are not the strength of all Christians. There are Christians who struggle with morality as others do with drinking or gossip. For such Christians they must determine before the Lord to set boundaries for themselves beyond which they will not go as it pertains to socializing with the opposite sex.

In addition, it must be understood that every man and every woman is susceptible to the lust of the flesh, the lust of the eyes, and the pride of life. Therefore to manage or guard against infidelity such things as communication, intimacy, and general companionship must be met consistently within the context of one's own marriage.

I believe that infidelity dissolves marriage. However, in many instances that marriage can be rebuilt. To rebuild a marriage, a distinction must be made between an adulterer and an adulterous act. The latter refers to a situation in which the offending party is overtaken by lust and acts on impulse, committing the act of adultery. An adulterer, on the other hand, is one who has determined in his or her mind to cultivate a relationship outside the marriage for the purpose of adultery.

To survive adultery, the couple must face together, as honestly as they can, the true nature of their situation. It must be determined whether they are dealing with a carnal act or a willful attitude.

Second, they most choose and agree together as to what they are going to do about the situation. The offended mate must have the felt freedom to leave and divorce, or remain in the marriage. If it is agreed that there will be no divorce, the offending party must truly repent and the offended party must truly forgive.

Third, the couple must agree to work together over time and with proper counsel to rebuild the marriage. This means dealing with the problem or problems in the marriage that may have contributed to its failure. It must also include putting the offenses of the past behind them.

Infidelity involves betrayal of confidence, the violation and defilement of the marriage vows and bed. To survive it, one must be truly committed to the restoration of the marriage.

PART 2

THE
CHRISTIAN
HOME

CHAPTER 6

GOD'S ENABLING STRENGTH

Over the past thirty years I have married numerous couples, all of whom seemed to be good people in love with one another. Unfortunately, for a number of these couples, what they felt for each other when they married was not strong enough to sustain their relationship as time and circumstances changed.

There are more than a few Christians who are of the opinion that God selected their mate for them. As far as they are concerned the person they married was God's choice for them. In other words, these good folk believe that their marriage was made in heaven. While it may be true that marriages are made in heaven, they are lived right here on earth in the cradle of fallen humanity where there is an unfettered devil with his entourage of demons.

After much consideration of this matter, combined with a great deal of frustration over the evident conflict in many Christian marriages, I came to this conclusion: the durability of a marriage with happiness requires more than two good people who love one another. To have a marriage that lasts with happiness at its core, the couple must have the daily enabling power of God the Holy Spirit.

I am well aware of the fact that for more than a few saints the idea of involving the Holy Spirit in the marriage relationship is a bit extreme. Yet it is evident that for more than a few good people, marriage is a boring, frustrating and unfulfilling experience. This suggests to me that something more is needed to make it what God intended it to be. That something is the enabling power of the Holy Spirit.

While riding down Martin Luther King Boulevard in South Dallas on the way to my office, I began to pay particular attention to the number of liquor trucks that frequent the community, stocking and restocking the many liquor stores with various kinds of alcoholic beverages. There was no chance of any establishment experiencing a shortage with this constant replenishing.

It occurred to me that the people who are the customers of these liquor stores find in the content of the liquor something that stimulates their spirit in such a way that it causes them to feel and experience some things that they could not otherwise feel and experience. It was evident that they liked the experience.

I have thought further about the evident human need for the incorporation of another spirit into one's body. Indeed a spirit that could cause the individual to feel and act in a way that is not common to his/her natural behavior. Based on the number of people who drink liquor, I concluded that there must be in most folk a need to feel and experience a kind of spirit and energy that moves them beyond themselves. In this context of thinking about the evident general human need for some kind of liquid spirit to stimulate the human spirit, my mind moved from the liquor stores and their stock of liquid spirits to the church house and our emphasis on the Holy Spirit.

There is a parallel between what a person gets from the liquor store, namely, liquor and drugs (spirits) and what a person gets from the church, namely, the Holy Spirit of God. They are alike in that they both stimulate the inner spirit of the person who ingests them.

I think that people who drink liquor and take drugs to the point that they are controlled by them do so for various reasons. Some see it as an avenue of escape; others need a stimulus to "face up" to something. Many want to feel a certain way, behave differently or verbalize something. Their natural spirit inhibits them. They need something more than what is naturally possessed to get them where they feel they need or want to be.

So it is with Christians. There is a need in our lives for

a spirit energizer that moves us out and beyond our natural spirit into an area of feeling and acting that is foreign to our natural selves. For the Christian that spirit is none other than the Holy Spirit of God. Ephesians 5:18 focuses on the need for human spirit stimulation in the lives of Christians. It offers an alternative to alcoholic beverages and drugs as that spirit energizer. "Be not drunk with wine wherein there is excess" (Eph. 5:18). The text is saying that for the Christian drunkenness is unacceptable. Note the fact that there is implied in this statement that even Christians need their spirits stimulated. However, the option for the Christian is not spirit stimulation by wine but rather, spirit stimulation by way of the Holy Spirit.

I find that a number of saints today have wet bars in their homes. In many instances these bars are fully stocked with different alcoholic beverages. I assume that for a number of Christians, men in particular, the road to relaxation is by way of alcoholic beverages. Unfortunately these men have not discovered the alternative to alcohol as a means of stimulating their human spirit and moving beyond their natural spiritual state.

In terms of spirit stimulation: the church is to the child of God what the liquor stores and drug dealers are to the indulging person. Both are sources from which one finds that which stimulates the spirit. The believer can no more stay away from the church in search of that spiritual stimulus than the drunkard can stay away from the liquor store in search of alcoholic stimulus.

The emphasis here is on drunkenness not drinking. Again the issue is not "to drink or not to drink," but drunkenness. The means by which the Christian can become drunk and thus controlled by it is either alcohol or the Holy Spirit. Both will produce the same effect: actions contrary to one's natural self.

On the Day of Pentecost the Holy Spirit came and filled the Apostles. Peter and the others began to preach Christ crucified and resurrected in the languages of all the people who were present. Those who knew them thought they were drunk. Peter responded to this by saying that it was too early in the morning for them to be drunk. They concluded that Peter was filled with the Holy Spirit of God. So when I say to you that there is similarity between the behavior of a person who is drunk on alcohol and the person who is filled with the Spirit, I am in good company. The difference is in the cause of the behavior and the nature of the behavior.

Attached to drunkenness is the phrase "wherein there is excess." Not only does alcohol cause the person to act in ways contrary to their natural behavior, but that behavior is characterized by excess or debauchery. To understand the concept of excess or debauchery in Ephesians 5:18, one may look at the prodigal son who wasted both his life and his money (Luke 15:11-32). He lived a life of excess. On the other hand, Acts 2 is an example of what behavior is like when one is filled with the Spirit. It is a life of extraordinary behavior . . . controlled, in order, no excesses.

In conversation with a number of women, I have heard many times that their husbands are more conversational, compassionate, and physically expressive when they have been drinking. These men use alcohol as a means of moving themselves beyond their natural way of thinking and acting towards their wives. For the Christian husband the alternative to alcohol as a stimulant is the filling of the Holy Spirit who indwells the heart.

The command for the Christian is to be "drunk" on the Holy Spirit. To be filled with the Holy Spirit is to be controlled by the Spirit in the same way that excessive wine controls the one who drinks it. Some think that being filled with the Holy Spirit is being saved. These people also think that the evidence of a Spirit filled life is found in the ability to speak in tongues. Such is not the case. The filling of the Spirit is about energizing the human spirit so that the believer is able to feel, think, and act in ways that are contrary to his/her natural human spirit.

The beer commercials on television are filled with images that set before us the notion that this or that kind of beer will enable young men and women to feel and act in ways that are more than a little bit exciting. It could well be said that a day on the beach is not what it could be without a trunk full of cold beer. Football and other sports are not as exciting to watch without liquor. Sex is not as intense without the enhancement of potent beer. Thus, the alcoholic beverage industry has reached a multimillion dollar level.

Let me carefully make the comparison that the church needs to emulate the liquor industry and advocate that life is not all that it can be without the enabling influence of the Holy Spirit on our human spirit. "Be not drunk with wine but be filled with the Holy Spirit," the text says.

The Spirit-filled life is not easily concealed. It will show up in how the believer behaves in public and in private. The Spirit-filled life has two significant effects on the believer. First, it enables believers to live life wisely rather than unwisely. Second, it enables believers to have and maintain a life of praise and worship of the living God. Three signs of a Spirit-filled life are found in Scripture. Ephesians 5:19-21 says, "Speaking to one another in psalms and hymns and spiritual songs, singing and making melody with your heart to the Lord; always giving thanks for all things in the name of our Lord Jesus Christ to God, even the Father; and be subject to one another in the fear of Christ."

First, we must note that being filled with the Spirit is a command from God to every believer. It is the believer's choice to obey or disobey this command. But for every believer who elects to be filled with the Spirit of God there is the experience of not being depressed or down in his/her spirit. The Spirit-filled child of God is one who is "up" on the inside. The Spirit of God, when controlling the human spirit of the believer, elevates the mind of the believer above circumstances. In spite of any current adverse situation one might be in, he/she is able to encourage others and sing praises to the living Lord. When the Spirit of God is controlling your life you will have a melody of praise in your heart to the Lord and you will be a source of encouragement to others.

The command to be filled with the Spirit is in the present passive tense. This means that in terms of being filled with the Spirit, no effort is necessary on the part of the believer. Rather, the believer must yield his/her mind to the power and influence of the Holy Spirit.

The "singing and making melody with your heart to the Lord" is not the way the believer rises to the point of being filled with the Spirit. No, this singing and making melody in the heart is the result of believers being filled with the Spirit.

The second sign of a Spirit-controlled life is an attitude of thankfulness to God for all the various circumstances that one experiences from day to day. The Spirit of

God enables Christians to trust God to always do what is best for them. The Spirit of God causes believers to believe that whatever it is that God allows to come into their life it is for their good no matter how it appears at that moment. Thus, there is the consistent attitude of thankfulness.

Third, the Spirit-filled life is a life characterized by a spirit of submissiveness. Stubbornness is not the way of life for the Spirit-filled believer. I take it that the Spirit-filled child of God is one who yields his/her will to the will of another believer.

The filling of the Spirit is tied to the challenge of both living the Christian life and doing effective ministry in the context of an evil and perverted generation. To the extent that we the church recognize the impossibility of our meeting the challenge of living and serving the Lord effectively and consistently . . . to that extent we will yield ourselves to the power of the Holy Spirit within us.

I am of the conviction that 2 Corinthians 6 forbids a believer to marry an unbeliever. This prohibition, however, must not be understood to mean that marrying a believer guarantees longevity and happiness in a marriage. It is possible for two believers to be married and not have a Christian home. Marriage to a believer is nothing more than God's starting point or the foundation upon which a lasting Christian home can be built. The key to this building process is the enabling power of the Holy Spirit in the lives of the Christian couple.

CHAPTER 7

A THEOLOGICAL
PERSPECTIVE:
BEING FILLED
WITH THE SPIRIT

There is some confusion about the concept of the
Spirit-filled life that needs to be addressed before I proceed
with explaining what it means to be filled with the Spirit.
First, let me list a few of the ministries of the Holy Spirit:

1. The convicting ministry of the Holy Spirit which
   relates to the unsaved (John 16:8-11). This is a
   pre-salvation ministry that convinces the sinner
   of sin, righteousness and judgment.
2. The indwelling ministry of the Holy Spirit which
   happens the moment the sinner is brought to faith
   by the Holy Spirit (1 Cor. 3:16).
3. The baptism of the Holy Spirit which happens the
   moment the sinner is brought to faith by the Holy
   Spirit (1 Cor. 12:13).
4. The leading of the Holy Spirit which guides the believer in his/her walk with the Lord. (Rom. 8:14).
5. The sealing of the Holy Spirit which happens at
   the moment of salvation giving the believer the
   eternal security of his salvation (Eph. 4:30).
6. The grieving of the Holy Spirit which deals with
   sin in the believer's life creating conviction (Eph.
   4:30).

7. The many and varied gifts of the Holy Spirit which equips believers to do the work of the ministry (1 Cor. 12–14).

Some Christians confuse the filling of the Holy Spirit which has to do with the believer's walk with God, with the indwelling of the Holy Spirit which has to do with the believer's positional relationship with God. Every believer has the Holy Spirit within him (Rom. 8:9, 10) and does not need to seek Him. While every believer is indwelt with the Holy Spirit, not every believer is filled with the Holy Spirit. Whether or not a believer is filled with the Holy is a matter of their own decision to yield to the Holy Spirit moment by moment.

In Ephesians 5:18 the command to every believer is to be filled with the Holy Spirit. To be filled with the Holy Spirit means the same thing as it means to be intoxicated with fermented grapes or an alcoholic beverage like wine. Therefore this command could read, "Let the Holy Spirit who is in you control your thinking and actions the same way that alcoholic beverage controls a man when it is in him."

This command is to all Christians and is therefore the obligation of every believer. It is not possible to be saved apart from the Holy Spirit coming into the heart of the believer and indwelling him the moment he believes. Nor is it possible for the Christian to live holy apart from submitting himself/herself to the control of the indwelling Holy Spirit.

There is only one verb in this entire section beginning at verse 18 and continuing to 6:4—that verb is "be filled." In each of the following statements in the Greek text, the participle is used instead of the verb, This is important to note because the participle gets its action from the verb. Thus, the verb "be filled" gives action to every participle in this long paragraph. We can understand the passage to mean that a person who is filled with the Spirit speaks to others in psalms and hymns. He sings and makes melody in his heart to the Lord. A Spirit-filled person is consistently thankful. A Spirit-filled person is submissive to other believers. The evidence of a Spirit-filled life is a spirit of worship and encouragement, an attitude of gratitude, and a spirit of submissiveness.

CHAPTER 8

GOD'S SUPER WOMAN: EPHESIANS 5:22-24

There are few things that I am more privileged to write about because of its importance and relevance than the relationship of a wife to her husband. I am convinced that the family is second in the mind of God only to salvation in terms of importance and relevance.

Some seem to think that in order for a man and his wife to have a happy family relationship, they must have grown up in an ideal family situation. Well let me tell you a few things that may be interesting to note. First, I want to call attention to the fact that, Mary, the mother of Jesus was accused of being a morally loose young woman by the religious community of her day. She was with child before she and Joseph were formally married. Second, Jesus Himself grew up in a stepchild-stepfather situation. In other words Jesus grew up with a stepfather. To be sure, this was not an ideal family situation.

In addition, there is listed in the family line (genealogy) of Jesus a prostitute (Rahab), and a polygamist (King David). These were not people with perfect life experiences, but they were part of the family line of Jesus.

When we think nostalgically about family we must get over our love affair with our idealistic past. Until recently, few people would admit to growing up in a dysfunctional family.

The African American woman has evolved from the

stereotypical Aunt Jemima to the blues-singing, male-dominating, bridge-over-troubled-waters type to the stereotype of a high living, bacon bringing home, pan-frying, man-satisfying, "she's gotta have it" type. This kind of woman is to be the mother of the children and the foundation of the African American families.

I have entitled this chapter "God's Super Woman." The term "super woman" is intended to call attention to the high regard I have for African American women. The strength and nobility of the African American woman is well-documented in the history. Women like the ebony-hued field hand, the high yellow "housegal," Harriet Tubman, Mary Bethune, ordinary maids, cooks, Rosa Parks, and a host of other women who, in spite of and in many instances because of the horrid social context in which they lived, demonstrated what I call super woman type abilities in the contributions they made to the struggle of African American people in this country.

However, my focus here is on the thousands of African American women who are content in their own homes and excel in their professions despite the impossible odds they faced. These women attained their greatness in the constructive character-shaping contributions they made to their sons and daughters in a society that demanded more of them than any ordinary woman could supply. Many of these women achieved strong professional credentials, rose to the top of their respective vocations, were the primary wage earner in their homes, lived at an economic level below what they could afford, and maintained a marriage relationship with a husband who is significantly below their level of achievement. Such women merit high praise.

The super woman is not only to be highly regarded for her social and professional achievements but she is also a woman of significant spiritual commitment. This is a woman who does not feel compelled to assert her independence as a woman, though she is thoroughly equipped to live independent of her husband. She chooses to yield herself to the Spirit of God and submit to her own husband.

After reading one of my books, a good friend of mine called my attention to the fact that I spoke frequently of my mother and not often of my father. I told my friend that my father and mother were married for thirty-five years until he died. I loved my father very much. However, it was my mother who worked all day in the fields with my dad, came home, cooked supper, fed the children, put us to bed, cleaned the kitchen, and then met my father's needs. More importantly, my mother shaped my heart and established in me a strong moral character on her knees. Without the super woman who was my mother, I seriously doubt that I would be who and what I am today.

It seems to me that for the African American family there is a need for a new assessment of just what this family thing is all about. For instance is the family a thing that has to be? Are there some alternatives to the nuclear family lifestyle? Is there and should there be a difference between white and African American families? Does Christ really make a difference in the stability and happiness of a family?

I think that there is a serious conflict in the African American family between the African American male and the African American female. The heart of this conflict is the social and economic redefining of the role of the African American women in which she emerges as the primary bread winner and part-time mother and homemaker in her marriage relationship with here African American husband and children. Let me point out again that in America today the African American woman is the second highest paid worker, following white men.

Come with me to the text before us today and notice the words, "Wives, be subject to your own husbands as to the Lord" (Eph. 5:22-24). It seems to me that the idea of being subject to another person is inherently repulsive because it gives the idea of being inferior to that person.

The subject of submission often raises the question of equality. That is to say that for more than a few men and women, the woman is not designed by God to share equality with men intellectually, emotionally, physically or economically. Thus the idea of submission to the husband is interpreted to mean submission to men in general.

For the record let me say to you that it is not possible to prove that women are inherently inferior to men in any area of their lives. There is equality between men and women in the full scope of their relationships.

To understand the focus of this passage we must note again verse 21 which says, "be subject to one another in the fear of Christ." I take it that the text is saying that in the church there is a spirit of humility which prevails so that believers are inclined to yield their will to the will of others. The Christian's idea of submission is not a mere wife-husband thing but a Christian-to-Christian thing.

So when the passage says to the wife "obey" your husband, it is instructing her to practice in her marriage relationship the same thing she practices in her church relationships. In addition, the obedient wife is obeying a husband who himself is given to yielding his will to the will of others including his wife.

I have two daughters. My wife and I did not raise our daughters to be submissive. In fact we did our best to raise them so that they would be as independent as possible. The reason we did not raise submissive daughters in the biblical sense of this text, is because submission to a husband is a spiritual thing—therefore can only result from the choice of our daughters to walk with God.

We must note the text carefully here for it sets before us God's idea of the marriage relationship as His earthly model of the relationship He has with the church. Whatever the nature of the relationship is between Christ and His church the marriage relationship must be contained and reflected in that same reality.

The text says that the wife is to obey her husband in everything. This choice of the wife to willingly surrender her will to the desires of her husband is not related to the strength, genius, or status of the husband. The decision of the Christian woman to obey her husband is nothing more nor is it anything less than her spiritual service to her Lord and Savior. This spiritual service that the Christian wife renders to the Lord by obeying her husband is based on her respect for God's divine arrangement of the structure of the family.

In the mind of God as He structured the family, He placed the man as the head of the family in the same way that He (Jesus Christ) is the head of the church. Just as the church submits to the will of Christ who is its head so the wife submits to her husband as her head.

One of the first things a male child learns is that girls are to do what they say. It does not matter whether they are right or wrong, "just do what I say and things will be alright." When the young man gets his first girlfriend, his long-term interest in her is most often proportionate to his satisfied need to control her mind and behavior. By the time boys become men, they have long since concluded that a good woman is one who knows how to treat her man which means doing what he tells her to do.

The young husband then comes to the marriage altar fully intending to control the woman he is marrying. The longevity of the marriage and whatever happiness it contains is most often reflective of who it is that is in control of things at home, him, or her. The husband who for whatever reason, does not or cannot control his wife will be frustrated and will vent his frustration in some destructive way.

What most men and women, husbands and wives seem not to consider is that marriage is God's plan; it is not merely a human idea, it is a God's idea. This means that the wife who is able to yield her will to the will of their husband is a woman who is being controlled by the Holy Spirit. The man who is the recipient of this kind of obedience from his wife is a husband who places such a high priority of spirituality and his walk with God that his wife feels his love, protection, provision, and affirmation just like every Christian feels those things from Christ.

Obedience that is the fruit of respect and humility is the rich product of a spirit-filled life on the part of both the husband and the wife. My teenage son and I go shopping from time to time; and as we walk the malls, I often watch him watch girls. As we pass young women in the mall my son will from time to time look at me and say, "nice tush." He sometimes says, "nice face." Every once in a while he will simply say "naaa." In all of these comments I recognize that my teenage son is merely acknowledging the externals of these young women. My role is to teach him that the real person lives inside that body and unless that person inside that body is saved and learns to let the Holy Spirit control her spirit, the exterior will not be worth having, regardless of its beauty.

CHAPTER 9

BEFORE YOU SAY YOU WILL, BE SURE YOU CAN

In Ephesians 5:22 the text reads, "Wives be subject to your own husbands as to the Lord." The words, "be subject" is written in italics in the New American Standard Bible which means that it is not in the original Greek text. This is important to note because it takes us back to verse 21 where it is stated that all Christians are to be submissive to one another. Such an attitude will facilitate positive relationships between Christians.

This same attitude of submissiveness that is to exist between all Christians is to be specifically applied in the attitude of the wife towards her own husband. However, it is well to note that in the Christian home the wife is not the only one who has a submissive attitude; every Christian in the household has the same spirit of submissiveness towards each other. Yet the wife gives particular attention to obeying her husband.

This attitude of submissiveness towards the husband is rooted in the wife's spiritual life. It is the Spirit-filled wife who is able to have and maintain an attitude of submissiveness towards her husband. This submissiveness on the part of the wife has nothing to do with the wife's abilities, intellect, or talents. The wife stands equal with the husband in these areas and she stands equal with the husband spiritually. This attitude of submissiveness as stated in this text is that of the wife's spiritual responsibility. She is to be submissive to her own husband as unto the Lord. This means that such obedience is a spiritual act. Such an attitude is beyond the reach of a wife who is not consistently filled with the Spirit.

The evidence of a Spirit-filled life is an attitude of worship, speaking to one another in psalms and hymns and spiritual songs, singing and making melody with your heart to the Lord; an attitude of gratitude, always giving thanks for all things in the name of the Lord; and having an attitude of submissiveness to others. The wife in whom these things are evident can be submissive to her own husband. Submissiveness is beyond the reach of the wife who is saved but not Spirit-filled. The reason the wife is to so treat her husband in this manner is because God made the man the head of the wife. The question of why God made the man the head is a question that only God can answer. He just did it; it had nothing to do with merit. It had only to do with His choice. It was God's choice and God's choice alone to make the man the head of the wife. God did not consult with anybody about His decision; He just did it.

This headship must be understood in the context of headship among equals. The man is the head of the wife in the same way that Christ is the head of the church (Col. 1:18, 24). Jesus is our head and yet we are His equals in that He is our brother and we are joint heirs with Him (Rom. 8:15-17). The husband is the head of the wife in the same way that God is the head of Christ (1 Cor. 11:3). God is the head of Christ, yet God the Father and God the Son are equal. So we must understand that when the Bible says that the husband is the head of the wife, it is not saying that the wife is not equal with the husband. This is headship among equals.

The headship that Christ holds in the church is not something that He received by delegation. The text says that He is the head of the church; but it also says that He Himself is the Savior of the body. I take it that this statement looks at the redemptive work of Christ which He did as the head of the church. As Savior of the body, Christ is the protector of the church. It is Christ who said that the gates of hell shall not prevail against the church (Matt. 16:18). The head of the church is what Christ is and as such He Himself prevents the enemy of the church from prevailing against it. In the same way, the head of the wife is what the husband is and as such, the husband is to be the protector of the wife. This means that the wife is to expect the husband to be her protector. To act independently of the husband is to put herself and her family at risk as did Eve in her encounter with Satan in the Garden of Eden.

There are three reasons in this text why the wife is to be submissive to her husband: First, it is her spiritual responsibility; second, God made the husband the head of the wife; and third, as the head, the man is the protector of the wife. Based on these three dimensions of the husband's relationship with his wife, the wife is instructed to obey her husband in everything.

The illustration of what it means for the wife to obey her husband in everything is found in the church's response to its head, Christ. The church lives in strict obedience to Christ. Whatever is the will of Christ, the head, is the will of the church, the body, His bride. The church has no separate agenda from its head. The church is totally dependent upon Christ for protection and direction. I take it that the wife in her relationship with her husband is to be totally dependent upon her head, the husband, for protection and direction, To have and maintain such an attitude of submission in the context of equality with the husband is beyond the reach of the wife who is not filled with the Spirit.

CHAPTER 10

THE SUPER LOVER: EPHESIANS 5:25

I t is evident that there are a number of frustrated husbands today. I am not sure that I fully understand the nature of this frustration but I do know that it is very real.

The frustration that many husbands are experiencing today shows up in their relationship with their wives in a variety of ways, not the least of which is withdrawal and silence even in the midst of company. This silence that is produced by frustration often erupts into violence towards the wife and children. The growing number of abused women and children is evidence of this fact.

For a number of African American men the frustration is even greater in that they are ladened with societal expectations. They are to marry at an early age, have an undetermined number of children during the first few years of the marriage, and be a happy head of the family. This should occur although they might never have had an opportunity to see up close such a family. In addition, the African American husband is expected to function effectively as the head of his wife and family. Often he does not have the spiritual depth, economic capability, or social skills to execute the mandates of this position.

Ephesians 5:25 states, "Husbands, love your wives just as Christ also loved the church and gave Himself up for her." It seems that more than a few husbands are caught in the spiritual trap of trying to force their wives to submit to them and their headship without first understanding their role in the relationship as the head of the wife.

I do not believe that anyone would disagree with the statement that in our relationship with Christ our obedience to His will, as we know it, is motivated by what He has done for us. Ephesians 4:32 states, "And be kind to one another tender-hearted, forgiving each other just as God in Christ also has forgiven you." Clearly the message here about our willingness to forgive one another is because God has forgiven us. To be sure our response to Jesus our Savior is motivated by what He has already done for us:

Romans 5:8, "But God demonstrates His own love toward us, in that while we were yet sinners, Christ died for us." In the mind of every believer, there is no room for any question of the genuineness of the love of God for His children. He loved us when we hated Him.

Romans 8:32, "He who did not spare His own Son, but delivered Him up for us all, how will He not also with Him freely give us all things?"

Romans 12:1, "I urge you therefore, brethren, by the mercies of God, to present your bodies a living and holy sacrifice, acceptable to God, which is your spiritual service of worship." It is the mercy of God which the believer has experienced in salvation that is the basis of the appeal to the believer to surrender his body to the Lord as a living sacrifice.

The first order of business of a Christian husband is not to command his wife to submit to his headship and do what he says. Instead, the first order of business for the Christian husband is to demonstrate his love for his wife just as Christ demonstrated his love for the church.

The love for the wife is to be demonstrated for the wife without any consideration of how the wife who is the object of the love will respond. This is unconditional sacrificial love in which the husband loves his wife for who she is and nothing more.

The words in verse 25 says, "Husbands, love your wives just as Christ also loved the church and gave Himself up for her." The text is saying to the Christian husband that the standard by which you are to measure how much you love your wife is the standard of love Christ set in His expression of the love that He has for the church.

Just how much did Christ demonstrate that He loved

the church? Jesus, the text says, loved the church so much that He gave Himself up for her. Let me hasten to add that Jesus demonstrated this kind of love for the church at a time when the church not only did not love Him back, but could not love Him back. Jesus had sacrificial love for the church. He put His life on the altar of sacrifice for the good of the church.

There has never been a man who could love his wife at this level. It is simply impossible for any human being to do. Yet this is God's standard for every Christian husband with his wife. Since this is God's standard for every Christian husband, then it must be possible to do it. There is but one way a husband can attain to this level of love for his wife and that is through the filling of the Holy Spirit.

The text says, "Christ loved the church and gave Himself up for her." Note the connection between the love Christ had for the church and what He did for the church. He loved the church. He gave Himself up for her. The very nature of genuine love in any context demands action. In the context of husband and wife, the husband's love for his wife constrains him to give himself up or her.

It seems that most husbands are intent on forcing their wives to submit by the use of forceful methods. God has never done that for us His church. The husband who would have a submissive wife must command that kind of attitude and behavior in his wife by giving himself up for her. That is what Christ did for us His church.

Christ did not and does not force His will on His church. Jesus laid down what it was that was best for Him choosing to do instead what was best for us. The Spirit-filled husband does not force his will on his wife; he chooses to lay aside what may be best for him choosing rather to do what is best for his wife.

As Christians we all know that there are time when we choose to disobey the Lord and do what is evil in His sight. When this happens, does God come after us with brute force? He does not. Instead He appeals to us on the basis of His demonstrated love for us. The power of love is God's way with His church and must be the same for the husband and his wife.

It is the spiritual responsibility of the Christian wife to allow the Holy Spirit to so control her life that she is consistently submissive to her husband. It is the responsibility of the Christian husband to allow the Holy Spirit to so control his life that he gives himself up for the good of his wife.

There are no small number of husbands who believe that if they could only get their wives to submit to their headship, then they would be truly happy. With this in mind look at the text again. "That He might sanctify her, having cleansed her by the washing of water with the word" (Eph. 5:27). The love a husband has for his wife is, first, sacrificial in that he gives himself up for the good of his wife. Second, the love a husband has for his wife is a sanctifying love in that it sets the woman who is his wife apart from all others and unto himself as his very own.

This giving of Himself in love for the church by the Lord Jesus had a two-fold purpose. First He wanted to sanctify her. To accomplish the sanctification of the church, the text says He washed her with the word. In terms of the effective sanctifying work of Jesus in the lives of each believer, there is no question but that this work of sanctification is the result of Christ giving Himself up for the church.

In the relationship between a man and his wife, his relationship with her is to contain the kind of sacrificial love that has a sanctifying effect on her life. I am saying that a man's love for his wife is to be such that it contributes to her spiritual development. In other words, the spiritual life of the Christian husband's wife is to be much more holy because of his love for her. It should not be so that such a wife is holy in spite of her husband's relationship with her.

The second purpose that Christ had in giving Himself up for the church was to present to Himself a spotless church. The text is saying that Jesus knew the kind of holy perfection He desired in His church and He invested Himself in His church so that He could get exactly what He wanted.

In the relationship between the husband and wife the husband must understand that he is the benefactor of the quality of his wife's spiritual life. Thus his investment of himself in his wife must reflect what it is he expects her to become.

It can be said without exception that in the long run a man gets back from his wife exactly what he invests in her over time. The level of love that a husband demonstrates for his wife will in time either contribute to her developing into the kind of wife he wanted to have or in time his marriage will be such that he will regret ever having a wife.

As an African American male I come from a long legacy of men who pride themselves on their ability to love a woman. As a young man I knew the legacy but I also knew two additional things—I knew that I was not cut from the same fabric that my predecessors were and I knew that what my predecessors advocated as love was not what I saw in the Word of God. Having been married now for more than thirty years, I realize that the legacy of love to which I was exposed as a young man was all about the flesh connection without regard for the heart connection. I could not attain to the standards of the flesh connection in my relationship with my wife.

In time I learned the heart connection, but that connection required a level of love to which I could not attain. I was frustrated and resigned to live my relationship with my wife the best I could with what I had. Then I learned that I had an additional resource that was designed to get me where I should be in my relationship with my wife—the Holy Spirit. Learning to allow the Holy Spirit to control my spirit in my relationship with my wife has made the qualitative difference in my marriage in terms of happiness and fulfillment.

Hebrews 13:4, "Let marriage be held in honor among all, and let the marriage bed be undefiled; for fornicators and adulterers God will judge."

Malachi 2:14, "Yet you say, 'For what reason?' Because the Lord has been a witness between you and the wife of your youth, against whom you have dealt treacherously, though she is your companion and your wife by covenant."

CHAPTER 11

SHE IS MY LOVE:
EPHESIANS 5:28

In our society we consider the individual is more important than the group. Thus, we tend to think of our individuality often without any consideration of the group to which we belong. This cultural pattern of seeing ourselves apart from others is no less true in husband-wife relationships than it is in our relationship with other people. In general, husbands and wives tend to see themselves as individuals separate and apart from one another.

Many husbands think their wife belongs to them and is placed on par with other possessions to be enjoyed at will and put aside when the pleasure is over. These husbands view women as separate entities. Men tend not to see wives as a part of themselves. There is no small number of women who see themselves as objects of male pleasure to be used at will. There is a new generation of women who seem to have no concept of moral restraint and integrity and who tend to believe that sex is a means to get what they want. For this new breed of woman, the concept of love is all tied up in the physical activity of sex.

There are young men who have taken their language from movies such as "Boys in the Hood" and the lyrics of rappers and rolled them into the idea that women are indeed nothing more than bitches and deserve to be treated as such. In an environment permeated with such thinking, is it possible for a man to view a woman as he does his own body? Are women likely to see themselves as being one with a husband who thinks this way about them? The cultural custom of individualism is so much a part of our attitude and behavior is in direct opposition to what the Bible teaches regarding the nature of the relationship between a husband and his wife.

The Bible teaches that a man's wife is as much a part of himself as is any other part of his human anatomy. In other words, a man's wife is not his subject to be ruled over nor is she his property to be used at will. Rather she is to him what his body is to his soul. Thus, as the soul of the man guides the body so the husband is to guide his wife.

How much should a man love his wife? The Scriptures set forth two standards to which a husband is to aspire. First, he is to love her as Christ loves the church. This means loving the wife with a sacrificial love which compels the husband to lay his life on the altar of sacrifice for the good of his wife. To love the wife that much means loving the wife with a sanctifying love that sets the wife apart from the crowd and exalts her unto himself as his bride. The husband who loves his wife as Christ loves the church will receive a wife who is spiritually and emotionally mature. She will be to her husband in terms of satisfaction, what the church is to Christ.

The second standard by which a husband is to determine how much he should love his wife is his love for his own body. The Scriptures admonish husbands to love their own wives as their own bodies. They continue by saying that a man who loves his own wife loves himself. The idea of a man loving his wife as he does his own body may seem a bit strange in a culture that is trained to think of themselves as individuals, separate and distinct from all others. However, the idea is not strange at all when we remember the creation story. In Genesis 2:24-25, God told Adam and Eve that the two of them were in fact one flesh. In Matthew 19, Jesus discussed divorce and remarriage. The Word says that the two are one flesh. Thus, we must conclude that from God's perspective, a man who is married is spiritually, emotionally, physically, and physiologically one with his wife.

The relationship between Christ and His Church is the model for the relationship between a husband and his wife. In that analogy the church is the body of Christ.

Christ is the head of the body the church (Col. 1:18). The church is one with Christ as His body. The wife is one with her husband; the two are one body. The Scriptures tell us that no one ever hated his own flesh. As it pertains to how a man feels about his own body, the norm is that he loves himself. How he treats himself is evidence of that fact.

If a man loves his wife he loves himself. How a married man feels about himself is evident in how he treats his wife. A man who mistreats his wife is a man who will neglect and abuse his own body. "For no one ever hated his own flesh" (Eph. 5:29). There is evidence which suggests that there are men who seem to hate their own flesh. Proof is seen in the detrimental abuses to which they are subjected. A man who has no regard for the negative effect of his habits and lifestyle on his body will have little concern for how his wife is affected by what he says and does.

Since the norm is that a man does not hate his own flesh, then we must conclude that a man who does not love himself is not normal. Thus, there are men who have emotional, spiritual, and physiological maladies that cause them to think and act in ways that suggest that they hate themselves. Let me add that a man who does not love himself enough to take good care of himself, cannot love his wife and will not take good care of her.

There are men who are stricken with the virus of low self-esteem which causes them to dislike themselves. This paralyzing virus is so devastating that when the man looks at himself in a mirror, he does not like the person that he sees staring back at him. When he listens to himself on tape, he does not like the sound of his voice. This man is of the opinion that he is not attractive to others. He tends to believe that he is less of a man than other men. Such a man is hardly capable of loving a wife because he does not like himself. Until a man is able to love himself as he is, that man is incapable of loving a wife as she is. He will treat the wife with the same contempt and shame as he does himself.

I recently watched a young boy come into a meeting room and sit down off to himself. Shortly afterwards I noticed that he had his head down and looked dejected and uncomfortable. His mannerisms suggested that he felt everyone in the room was looking at him in a negative way. It occurred to me that this young boy who was hardly in his teens had already lost his self esteem which would have caused him to feel badly about himself even in a crowd. After observing this young boy for a while, it further occurred to me that this young boy would some day become a man who would marry a woman that he could never feel better about than he felt about himself.

There are men who seem to feel that they are not deserving of the best, so they selfishly deny themselves such common things as good food in proper proportions, adequate clothes and other basic necessities. They think that less is better, so they live their lives in the alley of self-imposed social, economic and emotional depravation. The woman who would be the wife of such a man must know that he cannot treat her better than he does himself. The man who does not like himself for whatever reason, will find it impossible to love his wife. Thus the extent that a man is stricken with the virus of low self esteem or selfishness that causes him to hate himself will also cause him to hate his own wife and treat her accordingly.

You see it is not possible to be the body of a man and not be impacted by what the head decides to do any more than it is possible to be the body of Christ and not be impacted by what He does. Whatever it is that the husband does, the wife will feel the impact of it because she is as much his body and is his own body. It is a "she-is-me" connection. Neither partner in a marriage relationship can apply the slang, "See ya, I wouldn't wanna be ya!" even in jest. They would have to be satisfied with "See ya, cause I am ya!" That's being biblically correct.

Ephesians 5:29 says that a man does not hate his own flesh, but he nourishes and cherishes his body. The word *nourish* is also used in a father-child relationship (Eph. 6:4). The word cherish is used in the context of a mother nursing her baby (1 Thess. 2:7).

A man who is whole and sound in mind, body, and spirit treats his body in a way to develop and maintain a strong healthy lifestyle. To nourish the body one must include such things as a proper diet, medical care, spiritual development, physical exercise, and sufficient sleep. In other words, a man knows and does what is necessary to take good care of himself.

The second word is *cherish*. It is my understanding that a man not only does whatever is necessary to stay alive and healthy, but he also treats his body with compassion and tenderness as a mother treats her nursing infant. This means a man does not deprive himself of the soft side of life, choosing rather to cuddle and satisfy himself as a mother does her infant.

The man who loves his wife as he does himself is a man who anticipates and meets the overall physical, emotional, spiritual, intellectual and security needs of his wife. Included in this provision is an attitude of compassion and tenderness with which the loving husband cares for his wife. This tenderness and compassion convey to the wife security and affirmation of her significance in the life of the husband.

It is not enough for a husband to tell his wife that he loves her. He must demonstrate that love by providing for her every need. It is not sufficient for a husband to provide for the physical needs of his wife. He must also say, "I love you." Some men still believe that material things given and received are the best way of demonstrating love. While tangibles are important, the most significant factor in marriage is the shared attitude of oneness.

When lecturing on parenting, I stress the need for a strong bond between a father and his son. One of my students asked, "Professor Lane, given what you have said about a father-son bond, are we freaks?" He added, "We have not had any of the stuff you have said is necessary for growing a healthy adult." I thought for a moment and then I said to the student, "The word 'freak' is a bit strong, but yet it is not unfitting for what we are. Most of us do not have a familiar pattern in our past that can serve as a blueprint to follow in developing our families." On second thought, I would rather use the word "anomaly." We do indeed deviate from the norm.

The good news is that in spite of the deficit in my background as it pertains to models in family living, God has brought me to the point that I can be all that he ordained that I should be as a husband and a father. The key is my relationship with him and my determination to be controlled each day all day by His Spirit.

I have sought to establish the truth that from God's perspective a man's wife is one with him. She is as much his body as is his own body.

CHAPTER 12

THE GREAT MYSTERY:
EPHESIANS 5:31-33

Recently I was asked if I grew up in a home that listened to Christian radio. I answered, "No, I did not grow up in such a home, but the home in which I grew up was given to raising hell, on a regular basis. My family was genuine, bonafide, old fashion hell-raisers and few people did it better."

I suspect that my family environment was not unlike a number of other families both then and now. There are not a lot of people who were privileged to be in a home where biblical principles were an integral part of their home environment. For most people, church was church and home was home and what went on in one had nothing to do with the other.

There is in the family backgrounds of all African American people a legacy of slavery in which the concept of family was disallowed. This legacy still impacts the attitude of African American men and women towards one another to this day. A sense of estrangement from one another lingers like a specter from that peculiar institution.

The legacy of the African American male's social, educational, economic, and spiritual deprivation is also a great problem for the African American family. These deficits create a power struggle between the husband and his wife. In this context, she has more advantages than he does.

It can be said that if things continue as they are in this country, there will be so few living and free African American men that the family will be in dire straits by the 21st century. While more than a few Christians are playing around in and with our success, the African American male gender is swiftly being wiped out by feeding on itself. There is a strange virus in the stream of the African American community that has given our men an unquenchable hunger and thirst for the life blood of his brother.

"For this cause a man shall leave his father and his mother and shall cleave to his wife; and the two shall become one flesh." This enigma may be explained by studying Genesis 2:18-25, where the Lord worked with Adam to prepare him for Eve. First in verse 18, God made the observation that Adam was alone. To say that Adam was alone is to say that in all of creation at that point in history there was nothing that corresponded to what Adam was. The second thing God noted about Adam was that this state of being alone without a companion was not good for Adam. Having made these two observations God determined to fix this situation by creating for Adam a person who corresponded to what the man Adam was.

Before correcting the condition that Adam was in there was another problem that Adam had that needed fixing. This problem was with Adam's own sensitivity to his situation. The problem was God knew Adam was alone and that was not good for him, but Adam was not cognizant of his state. He had no sense that his being without a companion was not good for him.

What did God do to create a companion for Adam? In creating a companion, God did not disregard the fact that Adam did not know that he was alone. In this case God's timing in terms of meeting Adam's need for a companion was tied to Adam becoming aware of this need. God does not provide a wife for a man who does not know he needs one.

To sensitize Adam to his situation God created animals and birds and allowed Adam to give names to each one of them. As Adam named each animal, he began to notice that in every species there were two, a male and a female. He also observed that the males and the females all corresponded to one another. When Adam finished naming the animals and fowl the Scriptures observe, "But for

Adam there was not found a helper suitable for him." This was probably the juncture which Adam became aware of the fact that he had no companion . . . he was alone.

Adam was aware of his state and that this was not good for him. He recognized that he needed a person who corresponded to who he was. God gave to Adam a corresponding helper. To create her, God put Adam to sleep, took a rib from his side and fashioned that rib into a woman. He then woke Adam and gave to him his helper. At this point the new creature did not have a name, nor did she have a recognized place in the life of Adam.

When Adam looked over this new creature he did for her what he had done for all the other creatures God had given to him—he named her. This new creature was different from all the other creatures in that this creature was not made from the ground as were the others. Adam recognized that this creature came out of him and said, "This is now bone of my bones, and flesh of my flesh; she shall be called woman because she was taken out of man."

It is in this context that the words come, "For this cause a man shall leave his father and his mother, and shall cleave to his wife; and they shall become one flesh." The focus here is the nature of the creative relationship that exists between a man and a woman and the coming together of that creative relationship in marriage. For what cause should a man leave and cleave? Succinctly put the woman is bone of his bones and flesh of his flesh. In other words, a man and his wife are one flesh. When the text says that "they shall become one flesh," it is a reference to the consummation of the marriage relationship through sexual intercourse.

What other ramifications are inherent in the "leave and cleave" mandate? One is that the husband-wife relationship has priority over all others. There is no relationship on earth that should be given higher priority than the relationship between a husband and wife.

This is a great mystery. The mystery is truth that God kept secret for a while and revealed it in latter times. In the marriage relationship the mystery is this: when the husband leaves his parents and cleaves to his wife, the two become one flesh. This paralleled or was analogous to the not yet revealed truth of the relationship between Christ and His church.

In the marriage between Adam and Eve, God concealed a truth to be revealed later. Now that the mystery of the church has been revealed, it is also disclosed that marriage is a reflection of the relationship between Christ and His church. The mystery is indeed great! Just think. God so exalted the marriage relationship that it was used as a precursor to reflect the relationship between Christ and His church.

Since the murder of O. J. Simpson's ex-wife Nicole, there has been a growing sense of concern for abused and battered wives. There has even been some concern for battered and abused husbands. This new focus on battered women at the hands of their husbands is good and right. There is no small number of men who batter their wives.

Someone has said that marriages may be made in heaven but they are lived right here on earth. In this context I want to call attention to the Gospel of Mark 10:9 which says, "what therefore God has joined together, let no man separate." Can it be said that God has joined together every marriage? Is there some other meaning here in this verse?

The focus here is on the institution of marriage not on the individuals who marry. The text is saying that anybody who chooses to marry is participating in a God-conceived idea, and God-ordained institution. God is the custodian of this institution of marriage. God Himself holds marriage in all of human society as the one institution that is essential to the survival of society. God holds marriage up before the whole world as the model of what the church means to Him.

It is in this context that the Bible says that marriage involves a third party—and that third party is God Himself. Therefore, it must be said that people who marry are entering into God's relationship. Marriage is God's idea. Thus, the Bible says to let marriage be held in honor by all and the marriage bed undefiled (Heb. 13:4). As God ordained it, marriage is not something that once entered, a person can leave.

CHAPTER 13

HE WHO SAYS "I DO,"
MUST ALSO KNOW HE CAN

In Ephesians 5:25 the focus shifts from the wife who has been instructed to obey her husband in everything to the husband who is the head of the wife. The command to the husband is to love his wife. This can only be done when the husband is filled with the Spirit. Therefore, the kind of love that God has in view is beyond the reach of a husband who is not filled with the Spirit.

The evidence of a Spirit-filled life is an attitude of worship, speaking to one another in psalms and hymns and spiritual songs, singing and making melody to the Lord. It is an attitude of gratitude, always giving thanks for all things in the name of the Lord and having an attitude of submissiveness to others. The kind of love that many men have for their wives hardly reflects this. My observation is that there is little, if any, difference in the kind of love the Christian husband has for his wife and the kind of love the unsaved husband has for his wife.

The kind of love that the husband should have for his wife is the same kind of love that Christ has for the church. How much did Christ love the church? He *gave* Himself for the church. This means that the husband who loves his wife is a husband who abandons his own needs for the good of his wife. In reference to Christ's relationship to the church, He Himself is the Savior of the body. This means that Christ gave Himself up on Calvary for the sake of the church. He did not do this to *become* the Savior of the church. He did this because He *was* the Savior of the church. Christ gave Himself up for the church so that He might sanctify the church, cleanse it by the washing of water with the word, present it in all its glory having no spot or wrinkle and being holy and blameless.

The husband's first responsibility to his wife is to love her as Christ loved the church. This means that the husband is to take his wife and invest himself in her. The first investment is what I call the sanctification step. This is engagement. The engagement means that the man has chosen the woman to be his wife and has set her apart from all other women. In addition, he removes her from all other men as one who is no longer available to them.

The second phase of the investment of love that the husband is to make in his wife is what I call the bonding phase. The focus of this investment is in the wife's emotional and spiritual wellness. The goal here is to ensure that the woman is a Spirit-filled woman. Not just saved, but Spirit-filled. The husband must himself be Spirit-filled and as such, work to help his wife develop into the same. Should she already be Spirit-filled, the goal is to bond together as Spirit-filled Christians.

Finally, the man marries the woman and in effect, presents to himself a woman who is all she should be as a Spirit-filled wife. The husband who loves his wife will find that his love will cause her to become the type of wife who is uniquely fitted to fill his needs in every way. To love his wife is to invest himself in her. To invest in his wife is to invest in that which is his own gift.

A standard by which a husband is to measure his love for his wife is stated in Ephesians 5:28. He is to love his wife as he loves his own body. The kind of love that a man is to have for his wife is demonstrated by how he provides for his wife and how he treats her. The man demonstrates his love for his body by nourishing and cherishing it. The man who loves his wife will promote her growth in every area, spiritually, emotionally, and intellectually. He will also think of her as one who is very dear to his heart.

The Spirit-filled husband is the man who loves his wife with a sacrificial love that is likened unto the love that Christ has for the church. He loves his wife with the kind of love that he has for himself.

CHAPTER 14

DADDY'S CHILDREN: EPHESIANS 6:1-3

The Bible frequently speaks on the subject of children as both a blessing and a heritage from the Lord. Psalms 127 and 128 set forth these truths very clearly. Children are, as God says, both a blessing and a heritage from the Lord. They are the strength and the wealth of a family's lifetime accomplishments. The Lord Jesus Christ in His earthly ministry frequently used the innocence of children to illustrate His message of humility and forgiveness. He always had time for children, and children felt comfortable with Him. All who enter the kingdom of heaven must have the attitude of a child (Matt. 18:3).

I have witnessed the lengths to which men and women will go to get children. I can even testify to the unusual childrearing practices they use once they have them. Children are indeed a blessing from the Lord, but it takes nearly a quarter of a century to raise a child into an adult.

The climate for most African American children is not conducive to optimum growth and development. More than 51 percent are born to girls who are mere children themselves, ill-equipped to parent. Unwanted pregnancies are numerous. Many biological fathers do not assume responsibility for their numerous progeny. More than a few children are born with multiple strikes against them. They may be addicted to drugs even before they are born. Many have low birth weight and fail to thrive. If they do survive infancy, they face ostracism due to a number of maladies (ADD, HIV, hyperactivity, retardation, etc.).

Added to this dismal picture are the birth options and alternative lifestyles that result in a plethora of home environments. A child can have more than one biological mother or father (surrogacy); having four mothers and two fathers is not inconceivable (artificial insemination and surrogacy). A child may even be raised by parents of the same gender. Some states have legalized adoptions for homosexual couples.

We have seen pictures of starving mothers in countries like Somalia, Haiti, and Bosnia. Mothers were shown wandering about searching for shelter and food, carrying their nursing babies in their arms. The babies were suckling from their mother's emaciated breast as they went. One of the saddest pictures I have seen is a dying mother clinging tenaciously to her child, trying to keep him alive.

It is said that in this country during slavery, some mothers smothered their babies, rather than allow them to live and become the property of cruel slavemasters. For them they made an ultimate, unselfish sacrifice. This picture of devoted mothers is just one side of the child-parent relationship. It shows love and sacrifice. The other side of this picture are mothers who kill their children for selfish reasons. This picture of extreme rejection of children by their parents is followed by the reality of the untold number of parents who neglect, mistreat, and abuse their children on a daily basis.

In emergency rooms of hospitals in our cities are records of thousands of innocent children, who are the victims of their mother's boyfriends. These are children who are beaten, maimed, and sexually abused by lovers. I was shocked to hear of the number of boys and girls who are sexually abused by fathers or stepfathers with the full knowledge of their mother. There are also the untold millions of fathers who live well themselves, but who contribute nothing to the welfare of their children.

When I look at the plight of children today who are the largest group of poor people in the richest country in the world, I cannot help but think that something has gone wrong. For while the starving mother in a poor country like Somalia, tries to provide her nursing infant with milk from her empty breast, a love-starved mother in

America drowns her two little children in a lake so that she can keep her boyfriend. Something is terribly wrong.

Parenting, like marriage, is God's idea. All of God's ideas are ideal. In this ideal idea of raising children, parenting is a process that necessitates two parents, the mother and the father of the child, together in the same house. To raise a healthy adult from conception to adulthood, which takes approximately twenty-one years, both parents must be involved in the process.

Single parenting, though a common reality in our day, is contrary to the divine ideal idea of parenting. Tragically, almost 51 percent of all African American children are growing up in single parent households. It is not impossible to raise a healthy adult as a single parent, but single parenting is not God's ideal.

Bears are said to be solitary animals. When the female bear is ready to mate, she is driven by her natural instinct to attract a male bear and attaches herself to him until the breeding process is complete. From the moment of conception to the birth and full development of the bear cubs to adulthood, the mother bear is alone with her offspring. All that the cubs need to know about survival, they learn from their mother. The only role the male bear plays in the parenting process is the impregnation of the female.

With human beings, the process is very different. The human baby is the most dependent of all God's creatures. He/she requires constant care. Emotional stability and survival skills must be learned from both parents. It is possible for a single man or woman to raise a well-rounded child equipped to survive, but it is highly improbable. The odds are against them. Children who do not have a mother and a father in their lives together in the same house are at a serious disadvantage.

When I was a boy I often heard my mother say, "If it weren't for you children, I would have left your daddy a long time ago." For many years I did not understand what she meant by that. Now having seen the damaged children of so many broken families today, I at last understand what my mother meant. Even though her marriage to my father had lost its glow and she felt she deserved more than he provided, she stayed. What our father provided for his children just by his presence, was reason enough for her to persevere. My mother knew that the nurturing process of children was a two-parent process.

In the United States, we have lost sight of God's ideal for parenting, even in the church. The church lost sight of God when it lost sight of God's ideal for marriage. When divorce became an acceptable alternative to a lifetime marriage commitment, parenting was in trouble. Today we do not have a clue about how to reach and reclaim African American men for the family. And this reclamation is imperative for strengthening the African American community. Books have been written, seminars attended, conferences held, highly publicized marches made, and rededications made. Still we totter on the precipice of destruction. I argue for a different though long-range solution to our dilemma. It is a better idea than the recovering of men from the heap of destruction. I advocate starting with the children and raising them to be healthy adults, instead of repairing old men.

Another factor in the parenting breakdown is the state of the world. We are witnessing the beginning of the end of the world as we know it. People have lost their taste for Bible teaching, and have fallen in love with themselves. Their desire for religion is one that promotes self-love, one that turns a deaf ear except to their getting what they want for themselves, no matter who is hurt in the process. There is, in the churches today, a form of correct doctrine but no spiritual power.

The Scriptures are not silent; they provide instructions to children. They are admonished to obey their parents "in the Lord, for this is right." The instruction to children is the same as that given to wives. Obedience to the authority that God has placed over them is an expression of Christian service to the Lord. Second, obedience to parents is the right thing to do before God.

Colossians 3:20 states, "Children, be obedient to your parents in all things, for this is well-pleasing to the Lord." In this text the scope of obedience the child is to give to parents is emphasized. Obedience covers every area of the child's life. Such obedience is pleasing to the Lord. The child who obeys his/her parents must also honor those parents. The idea of honor refers to respect and value. The text is saying that children are to place a high value on the role and relationship that they have with their parents. Children who honor their parents have the promise from

God that they will experience longevity upon the earth.

Consider the story of Abraham, Sarah, and Hagar. All were involved in a conspiracy to help God fulfill His promise to Abraham. To this end Sarah, Abraham's wife, instructed Abraham to go to her maid Hagar and get her pregnant with the child God had promised them. Abraham took his wife Sarah's advice and got Hagar pregnant.

After Hagar conceived, she became proud, and Sarah became jealous. Sarah's envy resulted in Hagar being thrown out of the house before the baby was born. God found Hagar wandering about in the wilderness with no place to go, and sent her back home to Abraham and Sarah. After the birth of Isaac, Sarah and Abraham's long-promised child, Sarah instructed Abraham to throw Hagar out of the house along with Hagar and Abraham's son. This time they could not return home.

Here we have a single mother of an illegitimate child, abandoned by the system that produced her, left to fend for herself and her baby in the barren desert. It could be said that Hagar was caught in the trap of economic deprivation, without food, shelter and security. The man who knew God and had gotten her pregnant had concluded that it was better to send her away and get her out of his life. By sending Hagar and her son away, Abraham and Sarah were attempting to get rid of their mistake. They were trying to clean up their family mess.

Hagar in her moment of despair did not kill her child as she might have done. Instead she took her child and placed him in the best place she could find in the desert. Then she went a short distance away from the child and sat down, waiting for the crying of the child to stop, indicating that he had died. While Hagar waited for her child to die, an angel of God intervened and said to Hagar, "What is the matter with you, Hagar? Do not fear, for God has heard the voice of the lad where he is. Arise, lift up the lad, and hold him by the hand; for I will make a great nation of him" (Gen. 21:17-18). God provided water for them.

Young mothers, who are alone, lonely, in need and without hope, God hears when your child cries. To every mother who has a child who finds him/herself in need—to every lonely mother who finds herself in a place of abandonment, I say, remember God hears every whimper and He will see about that child.

CHAPTER 15

IT'S NOT OPTIONAL

There are instructions in Ephesians 6:1-4 regarding the attitude of the children towards their parents. The text has set forth the command to all Christians to be filled with the Spirit (Eph. 5:18). Again, the evidence of a Spirit-filled life is an attitude of worship, speaking to one another in psalms and hymns and spiritual songs, singing and making melody to the Lord with an attitude of gratitude, and having an attitude of submissiveness to others. It is the Spirit-filled wife who is able to be submissive to her husband. The Spirit-filled husband is able to love his wife as Christ loved the church and as the husband loves his own flesh. Likewise, the children are able to obey their parents only when they are filled with the Spirit.

Chapter 6:1 says, "Children, obey your parents in the Lord, for this is right." Obedience to parents for the children is a spiritual responsibility as is the obedience of the wife to her husband. In the Christian home both the wife and the children are in ancillary roles to the husband. Both are under the headship of the husband; however, the child is under the authority of both the father and mother.

The Spirit-filled child is to honor his/her father and mother which means that the child is to value his/her parents. The child puts a high priority on having a positive relationship with his/her parents. Those children who obey their parents will find life favorable to them and they will live a long time upon the earth.

As the father of a child who died at seven, I am not

sure that I understand this promise. However, the text clearly establishes a connection between longevity and respectful obedience to parents.

Every child has many basic needs, to which every parent must give adequate attention. In the context of communicating to children the idea that obedience to parents is not an option for any child, I will address one of those basic needs. Discipline is a basic need that every child has. It is in the context of discipline that children learn that obedience to parents is not an option.

Recently in a shopping mall in Dallas, Texas, two African American teenagers were caught burglarizing an African American-owned store by a few men from the Nation of Islam. The men from the Nation of Islam then caned the boys in the nude. The city of Dallas arrested the men for whipping the boys. The police were acting legally.

Interestingly, however, the response of the African American community to the caning was unexpected. For some African Americans, the action of the men from the Nation of Islam was consistent with the tradition of parenting in the African American community of years past in which the "growing' of children was a community project. There were others in the community, including the parents of these boys who thought such action by the men was nothing short of criminal. Ultimately the charges were dropped and the men released from jail. I would think that these boys, judging from the scars they carried from the caning, would hardly burglarize another business. The disciplining of these boys sensitized them to the fact that stealing was not an option.

At the center of the issue of the caning was the issue of discipline. Historically the African American parent has been strong on discipline when it come to children. The idea of discipline was a community responsibility. Apparently the Nation of Islam is still committed to that idea. The point is that when it comes to children, there are two things that are not optional. First, children's obedience to their parents is not optional. Second, parental discipline is not optional.

In my frequent trips to Israel, I most often go to the Wailing Wall and observe the Jewish Bar Mitzvah. This ceremony consists of Jewish fathers and their sons. Mothers are excluded. The ceremony takes place when the

boy reaches age twelve which traditionally signals the be-
ginnings of the coming together of mind, muscles, and
heart. In other words, it is about discipline. It seems that
Orthodox Judaism has a priority of discipline.

Most countries perceive discipline to be a basic need of
children. Yet in America such seems no longer to be true.
Today African American parents have lost sight of the
need children have to be disciplined,. Thus in many instances disciplining of children is perceived to be optional
in parenting. This has resulted in children concluding
that obedience to their parents is optional. The Scriptures
are replete with verses on the value of discipline in raising
children. Three main texts are:

Proverbs 29:15, "The rod and reproof give wisdom, but
a child who gets his own way brings shame to his mother."

Proverbs 22:15, "Foolishness is bound up in the heart
of a child; the rod of discipline will remove it far from
him."

Proverbs 23:13, "Do not hold back discipline from the
child, although you beat him with the rod, he will not die."

The results that Scripture promises as a result of discipline should be sufficient to encourage parents not to
treat the disciplining of their children as optional. The
method of discipline includes both corporal punishment
and verbal admonition. Parents who are consistent in
their discipline will find that the child will gain wisdom.
Wisdom is the ability to live skillfully. It is the ability to
distinguish between things, events, and ideas that seem to
be important and those that are not.

The parent who disciplines their child or children
will drive from the heart of the child the spirit of delinquency that accompanies the early years of the child's
life. Without consistent discipline the child will grow into
adulthood with their spirit of delinquency still in tact.

Third, the parent who consistently disciplines their
child will save his/her life as an adult. Proverbs 23:13
says that effective discipline rids the child of attitudes and
behavior that if maintained into adulthood can cost the
child his or her life. Lack of discipline produces a child
who will consider obedience to their parents as optional.

To speak of corporal punishment as part of effective
parenting in this day is to risk being classified as one who
agrees with the notion of abusing children. However, one

must consider what the Scriptures teach regarding the discipline of children. It is clear that discipline includes corporal punishment. But discipline must also include a variety of methods with the goal the same for each child. That goal is best summarized in Proverbs 17:6, "Grandchildren are the crown of old men, and the glory of sons is their fathers."

As a pastor who has the unhappy task of burying far too many teenage boys and girls, I have concluded that Christian parents must take seriously the admonition of the Bible in disciplining their children. The idea of discipline in parenting is equally as biblical as is the idea of children's obedience to their parents. Parents will discover that to the extent that they decide to treat the disciplining of their children as optional, to that same extent will their children tend to treat obedience to them as parents as optional.

CHAPTER 16

HEADSHIP AND THE CHRISTIAN HOME

Manage means to care for or to direct or carry on business or affairs. This basic definition denotes what is involved in a husband being head of his family. In 1 Timothy 3:4 one of the qualifications for becoming an elder is that a husband is able to manage his household well. So in Ephesians 5 headship can be defined as management. The husband has the responsibility of managing his family as the primary authority over his ancillary team—his wife and his children.

The manager of the household must have a vision for his family. This means having plans, goals, and objectives. He must be able to communicate in a positive way with those under his leadership. He must be able to inspire positive attitudes in his family. He must be able to protect them and provide for them. The affairs of the household must be in the custodial care of the husband who is the head with room for sharing and delegating some responsibilities as talents and abilities warrant.

As the head of the family there are several things that the husband must manage well:

1. He must manage the spiritual life of those in his household;

2. He must manage his relationship with his wife and children;

3. He is to oversee the discipline of his children;
4. He is responsible for the financial stability of his household;
5. He must manage the moral lives of those in his family;
6. He is to manage the emotional environment in his home;
7. He must manage the growth and development of his children; and
8. He must manage his and his wife's spiritual and emotional development.

It is evident in many marriages that the husband is not a good manager of the authority that God has entrusted to him. There are three extremes that seem to be prevalent among men in terms of their management. On one extreme there is the man who manages his authority like a dictator. Every decision is arbitrarily made by him and stringently enforced. At the other extreme is the man who uses the principle of laissez faire. Each member is left to do as he chooses. Then there is the manager who vacillates. He wavers indecisively between one course of action or opinion and another. Nothing is ever really settled.

Each of the three extremes produces negative results in family members. The wife and children are subject to the leadership of the husband/father. The husband who is a dictator will provoke his children to wrath and will evoke bitterness in his wife. The children of a man who is too lenient will disregard him and his wife will usurp his authority. The ambivalent manager only manages to contribute to the instability of the whole family.

Headship denotes a position of leadership. It connotes one of control. If one is to superintend he must be thoroughly knowledgeable of who and what he commands. I recently flew a few hundred miles at 10,000 feet in a small Cessna 402. There were eight people on this plane and I sat in the cockpit with the pilot. The pilot was quiet, soft-spoken, even-tempered. As we took off and got into the air it occurred to me that this mild-mannered man was not only in control of this plane, but he also was accountable for everyone in it. To do this the pilot had to have a thorough understanding of how much weight the plane could carry. Thus, he weighed each passenger and each piece of luggage.

The people and luggage had to be balanced in the plane. The pilot loaded the plane himself. He knew the location of every mountain in the area and their altitude. In aviation, the pilot is not only in control, but he is also the flight manager. The same is true of the husband—he is not only in charge; he is also the manager.

There is a disproportionate number of female-headed households in our community. In these homes the absence of a male in a leadership role contributes to a growing number of men who have no idea of what it means to manage a family. Consequently African American women are increasingly marrying men who have no vision for the future. These are men who do not know where they are going or how they will get there.

After observing men and women for three decades, I have come to the conclusion that African American women in general are better equipped to manage their families than are African American men. Factors contributing to this are: (1) women are doing most of the parenting in the African American community; (2) they are generally more educated; (3) they are more religiously involved, and (4) they have more social skills. Thus, in many instances the premarital counselor must equip the African American husband with the vision and skills necessary to manage a family. We must not make the mistake of thinking that salvation alone is all that is necessary to lead a family. In addition to salvation a man must have a vision for his family.

When a man chooses to take a wife, he is assuming the responsibility of managing another person who is totally different from himself and who brings to the marriage her goals and expectations. This is not an easy task. The birth of children adds a third dimension of managerial responsibility to the husband. For most husbands this is a considerable amount of pressure to have thrust upon him.

In the absence of good managerial skills the pressure from this deficiency produces in some men the extremes of over or under management. All to often, unfortunately, by the time the husband comes to grips with his management skills, he has seriously damaged his household. A damaged household normally means a dysfunctional home. This is the result of poor management of headship.

Ann asked Jim for a divorce saying, "We are not going

anywhere together and I refuse to live the rest of my life in this rut." Jim responded, "But I work hard and you have everything you want. What else is there?" As I listened to Jim and Ann struggle with their marriage situation, it was clear to me that the root of their problem was Jim. Although he was a good man, he had no vision for the future, and was ill-equipped to lead his family. Jim thought that his wife was fortunate; she had the best of all worlds.

The husband who does not manage his authority well will create consistent crises in his family and his inability to properly manage his authority will cause his family to fall apart. It is not possible to manage a crisis when one cannot manage in general.

CHAPTER 17

SUBMISSIVENESS AND THE CHRISTIAN HOME

he word subordinate denotes inferiority, sub-
servience, or a lower rank or class. Ancillary denotes the
same, but connotes supplementary, assistance, support . . .
help. Both have been used from time to time to refer to the
role of the wife and children in the home. Being in a lower
rank usually means that the someone who is over you is
your superior. Inherent in superiority is that idea that
someone is better or more important than the subordinate. In the marriage relationship, however, we must disregard the customary usage of the words. The conven-
tional usage assails the sensitivity of more than a few
wives and children.

In the marriage relationship the husband does not
rank higher than the wife and children as an individual
nor is he superior as an individual. As individuals they
are equals. The terms are only relevant in marriage as
designation of the role and the function of family members. The husband is the head of the wife by divine ap-
pointment. This is not a matter for debate. As the head of
the family, the husband is responsible to manage his
equal as his equal.

To be in a subordinate role as a wife means being under the managerial authority of the husband as an equal.
This means willfully obeying the husband as a matter of
spiritual responsibility.

There are three reasons in this text why the wife is to be submissive to her husband. First, it is her spiritual responsibility. Second, God made him the head of the wife. Third, as the head the man is the protector of the wife. Based on these rationales, the wife is instructed to obey her husband in everything.

Given the reality of family life, some wives are the victims of the poor management skills of their husbands. In such cases, the husband may be dictatorial, inactive, or too lenient. In either case, the result is that the wife develops a negative attitude towards her husband in particular and family life in general. In some instances, the wife refuses to function under the managerial authority of the husband. Consequently the whole order of the household is disrupted and unity suffers.

A lack of unity in the home creates a dysfunctional home (one that is impaired or functions abnormally). This is often the result of a husband who is ill-equipped to manage and a wife who fails to function in the role God commanded. The first priority in a Christian home is to be a Spirit-filled Christian. The evidence of a Spirit-filled life is a spirit of worship, encouragement, an attitude of gratitude, and a spirit of submissiveness.

Growing out of the Spirit-filled life is the ability to elevate the marriage beyond the level of the natural, to a higher level that is based on the relationship between Christ and the church. In the Spirit, the marriage relationship functions as it was designed to function when it is reflective of the relationship between Christ and His church. The Spirit-filled husband is a man in the process of becoming a good manager of the authority that God has invested in him as the head of the family. The Spirit-filled wife and children function as a willing ancillary team under the authority of their leader.

—————— PART 3

FAMILY
COMMUNICATION

CHAPTER 18

COMMUNICATION BETWEEN HUSBANDS AND WIVES

According to Webster, to communicate means to cause another to share . . . to be connected . . . to transmit or exchange thought. It is basic to human survival and it is vital to interpersonal relationships within the family.

I am convinced that there is a direct connection between the major reason given for divorce—incompatibility—and the lack of communication between couples. The term incompatibility has several meanings; however, the most common refers to couples who have grown apart socially. They cite evidence of their inharmonious state, "I've outgrown him/her. We don't have the same goals. We have nothing in common." In many cases, the facts will show that the real problem behind incompatibility is poor or negative communication between the couple. The quality of the communication between a husband and his wife is a sure barometer of the degree of the compatibility between the two.

A person's felt need for a corresponding helper is the catalyst that promotes communication, not shared interests. Having a companion fills the need to relate in a total way to one who corresponds to what a person is as a living human being.

Many professionals who are in the business of helping

couples, advise them to accentuate what they have in common. It is recommended that they invest substantial time and money in pursuit of those activities that they share. They are even told to feign interest in their spouse's hobby. Even if it bores them to tears, they should fake it. This idea that compatibility is built upon shared interests is a false assumption. Rather it is motivated by a need for a companion who as a human being must communicate.

One of the stereotypes of African American men is that they are better at initiating relationships with women than they are at developing and maintaining relationships. My experience as a counselor for many years tends to support this stereotype. It has been my observation that most African American men have what seems to be an innate ability to initiate conversation with women even in instances where there are serious differences in their social and economic status. However, once the relationship is initiated, that same man will waver in his commitment to develop and maintain it.

Brenda and Bob had such a relationship. Bob was the kind of man who seemed to be the main attraction of any group of women that he was around. At home he hardly talked to Brenda more than a few minutes. Brenda was seriously frustrated by his behavior. Bob's problem was that he found it difficult to share himself with anyone especially his wife. Bob's conversations with his many female friends were about them, not himself. Brenda wanted a relationship with depth. She sought to get inside Bob's head; he avoided what he viewed as an intrusion and used silence as a means of escape.

Some married people say that their mate will not talk to them about anything at any time. In these families there is the perception that communication is only that which is spoken. Words are just one form of communication. In these same families other forms of communication are functioning well.

Companionship is at the heart of good communication. To the extent that a person recognizes his/her need for companionship, it is to that extent that communication occurs with the mate. Many men and women are out of touch with their own emotional need for a companion. So in their marriage, they avoid feelings and utilize only that part of the mate that they feel they need. They have little sensitivity to the idea of companionship. It is possible in this context to be a mate without being a companion. A companion is one who shares his/her whole person with another not just some aspects of their being.

There are those who are best described as loners. These are people who have developed the kind of attitude which causes them to only feel a need for others in select areas. They usually do not have a felt need for a companion, but more for someone for specific things at certain times. These are people who are out of touch with their feelings in general.

There are many problems that tend to hinder the process of communication. One primary impediment to communication between husbands and wives is the problem created by the attitude of men toward women. It is one based on a female's value being tied to her physical attributes. This attitude is shaped during the preteen years of the average young man. By the time he becomes an adult, he views women only in superficial terms and expects them to meet his needs.

Boys first discover girls by physical attraction. This discovery is followed up by physical contact in the form of petting, and then sex. By the time boys become men, they have developed attitudes towards women that define their need for women in terms of the physical. As a result of this attitude, men tend to communicate with their wives at the physical level, often at the exclusion of the companionship level which includes other forms of communication.

Men and women are socialized to view relationships differently. While men tend to focus on the physical level with their mates, women on the other hand, tend to focus on the emotional element. Girls feel a great need for love. Since this need is often not met in the home by the father, at an early age, girls reach out to boys for affection. Most boys are willing to engage in sexual activities, which girls interpret as affection. As a result of these kinds of experiences, adult women will often communicate with their husband at this single emotional level.

With this kind of socialization gap, verbal conversation between the couple is not frequent. The missing ingredient is the felt need for companionship. In companionship there is the need on the part of the man for a corresponding helper, not just a body. The woman likewise has the felt need for a whole man not just his feelings.

My wife and I have two adult daughters, one of whom is married and the other is soon to be married. In raising our daughters, I found it necessary to limit my activities so that I could be available to fill the need in our daughters' lives to feel loved by their father. The pastorate lends itself to creative, flexible scheduling. Therefore, I was able to avail myself to them as needed. When our daughters began to date it was evident that they were loved by both their parents, thus they were not looking for a somebody to love them. I should add that the love I have for my daughters was reinforced to them by my evident love for their mother.

CHAPTER 19

COMMUNICATION BETWEEN PARENTS AND CHILDREN

The most essential asset in communication is the willingness and the ability to listen to what the other person is saying. Any parent who wishes to communicate with their child must learn to listen attentively to what that child is saying verbally, emotionally, and physically.

There are several roles parents play in communicating with their children. These roles may use nagging, reminding, criticizing, cajoling, threatening, lecturing, questioning, advising, evaluating, probing, or ridiculing.

Parents who communicate poorly with their children most often function in one or more of the following roles:

(1) Commander-in-chief—control/demands;
(2) Moralist—preaches proper feelings;
(3) Know-it-all—shows superiority;
(4) Judge—always right, child wrong;
(5) Critic—ridicules the child;
(6) Psychologist—analyzes child feelings; and
(7) Counselor—sympathizes/pities

The alternative to functioning as a parent in such roles in the parenting process is learning how to listen to the child and then responding clearly and precisely to what has been expressed. In responding, the parent should accentuate the positive and give a clear response to what they understand the child expressed. The name of this game is encouragement.

The parent who learns how to encourage the child and does it on a regular basis will find that their child will develop self confidence and a strong feeling of self-worth. Encouragement is one of the most effective ways of developing and maintaining a strong, positive relationship with children. Encouragement is the process by which the parent focuses on the assets and strengths of the child and seeks to build upon them. Encouragement is the means by which parents help their children prepare for and deal with mistakes. Encouragement helps a child develop the courage to become something less than a perfect person.

There are several ways that a parent can develop a means for positive communication with their children:

(1) Accept the child as he/she is with a view to what he/she could be;

(2) disregard the little negative things like tattling, choosing rather to focus on the positive things that the child does;

(3) trust the child to be who he/she is in your presence;

(4) recognize and accent the child's efforts and improvements and those things the child accomplishes.

Children need to see their parents as those who have confidence in and are supportive of them. Positive parents produce positive children. The reverse is also true. One of the most intimidating thing about being a parent is the realization that modeling is a means of communication, and as such children learn attitudes from parents. In spite of what we say many of the attitudes that children develop are reflective of the attitudes that are exhibited in the home. The child's concept of male and female sex roles are developed through their interpretation of what they see in the home. It is out of this concept that children shape the standards by which they will choose a mate.

A father who shares in the household responsibilities and leads the family will probably raise children who feel a part of the family as opposed to one who feels alienated from the family. Such a father communicates a sense of involvement by his example. A demanding father will most likely raise demanding children who may not be devoted to the family.

Because modeling is a means of communicating with children, it is essential that parents understand that the roles they portray in the home and in the community are the roles that the children will understand to be the norm. Unloving and uncaring parents should not expect to raise children who are loving and caring.

PART 4

CONFLICT
MANAGEMENT

CHAPTER 20

REBELLION AND BATTERING

It is difficult to believe, yet painfully true, that the little bundle of joy parents bring home from the hospital can, in a few years, become a nightmare to the whole family. I call this transition into terror: *rebellion.*

The two most descriptive examples of rebellion in the Bible are Saul in the Old Testament (1 Sam. 15) and the prodigal son in the New Testament (Luke 15). In both of these cases the spirit of rebellion was a thing of the heart and it caused the individuals to reject authority and act out their own will. Rebellion is the ultimate expression of selfishness and pride.

Rebellion is the kind of spirit that defies and resists authority. Thus any attempt at managing rebellion is reacted against by the rebellious person. In confronting rebellion, remember that it is evil, and not unlike the sin of witchcraft (see 1 Samuel 15:23). It has the power to destroy both the individual and whatever relationships they may have. It is the kind of attitude that puts the future of the one in rebellion at risk.

There are perhaps as many causes behind rebellion in children as there are causes behind rebellion in adults. However, in children, the most common cause is mismanagement of authority in the home combined with the absence of a spirit of submissiveness. A rebellious child is often an angry child. The anger may be caused by neglect by the parents. In some instances, the anger is caused by witnessing abuse between the parents.

One of the best ways to manage rebellion in a child is utilizing preventives. Parents must understand that rebellion is bound up in the heart of a child and specific discipline is required to drive it from the child's heart. The other alternative is little or no discipline at all. This leaves things to chance. therefore, it is far less reliable in predicting how the child will turn out. The best strategy is to balance rebellion with consequences in which the price of rebellion is more than the rebellious one can afford to pay. This method is illustrated in the parable of the prodigal son in Luke 15. Disciplinary actions that may be used to counter persistent rebellion are verbal chastisement, physical discipline, loss of privileges and, finally, eviction from home.

One of the fundamental causes behind rebellion in teenagers is an unstable, insecure, early childhood in the midst of a hostile environment. These children who cannot be sure of consistency in having their daily basic needs met learn fear. This fear turns into negative defense strategies. These unmet needs may be as basic as love, safety, shelter, food, and clothing. They must be met. Parents also need to nourish and protect their children's emotions and spirit. They need to spend time hugging and playing with them. They also need to nurture their hearts spiritually resulting in their turning to the Lord at an early age.

To manage rebellion parents must build the communication tie between themselves and their children. They should be able to talk honestly and openly with one another. During this open communication parents demonstrate that they have clearly established convictions and values that they want to pass on to their children.

The key to understanding rebellion in a child is understanding the cause behind the rebellion. It has been my observation that by the time many African American boys reach their teens they are in full-blown rebellion against their father. This same pattern seems to prevail between mothers and daughters. A primary contributing factor in this kind of rebellion is a negative relationship between the mother and father. The man who batters the mother of his children will in time face a rebellious son. A mother who disregards the authority of her husband will in time face a rebellious daughter.

I remember well the day Shelly learned that she was pregnant. She could not have been more excited. The day Bobby was born was a day of excitement for Shelly and her husband. As he grew up, the bond between him and his mother could not have been stronger. I noticed, however, that the older Bobby got the more he withdrew from his father. By the age of fifteen, Bobby had grown as large as his father and was in full-blown rebellion. I came to understand in counseling sessions that Bobby had been born into a home in which verbal and physical abuse was the family secret.

Physical and emotional battering refer to conflict between a husband and a wife that involves beating one another. One is felt externally, while the other internally. In reality, both physical and emotional fighting are a form of communication. It is negative communication to be sure, but it is communication. There is a third form of emotional battering called silence. This is the refusal to communicate verbally with the mate. When the method is silence, the body language is the means of communication. It is commonly thought that people who fight with words, fists or silence are mean people; they may be. However, a more accurate description of such people may be selfish, insecure and poor communicators.

Such was the case with my mother and father. They seemed to love each other all of the thirty-five years they were married, until my father's death. Yet they often fought with fists and words. Sometimes the war would go on for hours before peace emerged.

As a child, it seemed strange to me that two people could still love one another and fight as my parents did. When I became a man and observed that same behavior between them, I discovered that my father was seriously limited in his ability to communicate. He stuttered, swore, and was functionally illiterate. Because of this, he never learned how to develop and maintain positive relationships. Not even he and his siblings got along. Thus fighting was the only way he knew to assert his will over my strong-willed, literate, articulate mother.

People who fight are saying to the object of their hostility: the price of resisting my will is for you such a painful experience it would be better for you to let me have my way with you. In other words, do not resist my will or I will hurt you.

Abuse in the family creates the worse kind of crisis in the home. It must be dealt with in a way that solves the problem. To manage abuse in the family, the abuser must be retrained to believe that the domination of another person is not a right granted to anyone. The abused must realize that no one deserves to be abused. The object of abuse must understand the meaning of codependence and realize that the attitude and behavior of the abuser is not their fault. The only way to survive abuse is to stop it. No mate has the right to abuse another. There is no love in abuse. Abusers have little understanding of what love is.

Most abusers have themselves been abused, and they are in a cycle of abuse. To break out of that cycle, serious changes must be made in their life. This will determine how abuse is handled in the home.

There are few crises that a family faces that have a greater propensity for long-range destruction as does the crisis of family violence. Usually rebellious children are the result of a dysfunctional family environment in which the family is in conflict within itself. The primary cause behind rebellion in children is usually abuse and rebellion in the experience of the parents.

To break the cycle of abuse and rebellion, families must find ways to reprogram themselves so that they can communicate in positive, constructive ways. This may mean dealing with the unfinished business of interpersonal anger towards authority carried over from childhood. This normally involves four steps: (1) Work at understanding who you are as a person newly created in Christ Jesus; (2) learn to like yourself and work at developing your own self-esteem; (3) develop strong ties with others and promote their self-esteem; and (4) work at becoming a clear, positive communicator.

CHAPTER 21

A FATHER WHO FATHERS: EPHESIANS 6:4

I n the context of the African American community it is not unusual to find a strong and lasting bond between the African American mother and her sons. This bond is in more than a few instances stronger than the bond between that same woman and her daughters.

In an article published sometime ago entitled "Black Men, An Endangered Species: Who's Really Pulling the Trigger?" The author said, "Black parents should spend more time raising their male children. In many families sons do not receive the nurturing that their daughters receive. Boys are allowed too much freedom to decide their life-style, educational goals, and careers. As a consequence, many Black men never reach their full potential. Black parents, especially fathers, must invest more quality time and energy in raising sons."

I am in full agreement with this author. There is overwhelming evidence that the modern day African American parent is producing underdeveloped sons who must live in a fully-developed society. Let me cite a few facts that we must not overlook:

(1) African American youth have a 50 percent higher probability of dying before age twenty than any youth of other ethnicities in this country.

(2) The major causes of death of African American youth are homicide, drug abuse, suicide, and accidents.

(3) Thirty percent of all African American youth in America drop out of school before ninth grade

(4) Forty-two percent of all homicide victims in America are African American and most of the perpetrators are African Americans.

(5) Only 33 percent of African American youth go to college after graduation from high school.

In terms of parenting, we may be doing quite well as individuals in our own homes, but as a race of people we are not doing well at all.

Ephesians 6:4 says, "Fathers do not provoke your children to anger." Colossians 3:21 echoes this: "Fathers, do not exasperate your children, that they may not lose heart."

In Ephesians 4:26-27 the noun παροργισμῷ is used in reference to unresolved anger, giving the devil an opportunity. Here in Ephesians 6:4 the verb παροργιζετε is used to warn fathers against provoking anger in their children.

To avoid provoking anger in their children, fathers must avoid attitudes, words, and actions which would drive a child to anger and resentment. Fathers must avoid excessive discipline, unreasonably harsh demands, abuse of authority, arbitrariness, unfairness, constant nagging, and condemnation. These subject the child to humiliation and demonstrates general insensitivity to the needs and value of the child.

Someone has said that a child should not be corrected by pain, but by persuasion. For some reason it seems that African American fathers believe the only way to correct their sons is by hurting them emotionally, physically, or economically. The idea seems to be that the correcting is in the hurting.

For many years, we have observed the African American professional athlete looking into the lens of a camera and saying sweet things to his mother. Seldom does the son of an African American man publicly express love or appreciation to his father. It seems to me that the fact is that not many sons of African American men either love or respect their father. The words that perhaps most accurately express the feeling of African American sons to their father are "anger" and "rage."

Leonard Pitts related an intriguing story in an article

published in the *Dallas Morning News* March 17 1995 entitled "Black Boys Need High Expectations." Mike was a "nigger" and because of that never would amount to much. He knew that, because his father often told him so. Greg was a white boy, and though he faced daunting obstacles, he could realize his dreams if he just worked hard. He, too was told that by his father.

You should not be surprised to learn that Mike drifted through the company of pimps, whores, thieves, and drug dealers. He was blinded in a bar room shooting in 1974. Nor should it surprise you to hear that Greg became a teacher and a lawyer, earned a Ph.D., and now is the dean of a law school.

What may surprise you though, is that they are brothers of the same parents. Their mother was white and their father was racially mixed and psychologically mixed up. He could not cope with being a light-skinned black man passing for white. Perhaps it was this self-loathing that caused him to encourage one son and revile the other, though both of his sons looked as black as Brad Pitt. This African American father learned a method of parenting that is inherently destructive. It turned one son into an angry child who grew into an angry man full of rage.

When I look back at my own childhood, the word that most accurately expresses the feelings of my brother towards our father is anger. It must have been true in the relationship between them that my father provoked my brother to anger. In that persistent provocation from my father, my brother lost heart and gave up trying to please my father.

Colossians 3:21b says, "that they may not lose heart." What does it means to lose heart? A child who has lost heart is a child who has a broken spirit. When a child goes throughout the day in a listless, moody, and sullen frame of mind, then that child is demonstrating the characteristics of brokenness.

Brokenness has at least three basic characteristics: (1) a sense of hopelessness crouched in a spirit of inward rage; (2) a loss of self-esteem embedded in an attitude of insecurity; and (3) a persistent state of depression combined with a fear of being alone.

It is totally within the reach of any father to so exasperate his children, especially sons, that they lose heart and become walking time bombs. A few years back there was a commercial jingle about Michael Jordan which said "I want to be like Mike." When was the last time you heard a son of an African American father say, "I want to be like my Dad?"

A former football player with the Denver Broncos talked about his past history as a wife abuser on a television show. He recalled standing over his father during a fight threatening to kill him because he repeatedly beat his mother. This man said that the anger that dominated his life was rooted in his hatred for his father. He was currently in his fourth marriage.

I am aware that African American men are not the only fathers who have sons who are filled with anger, but my concern is that it appears to be the norm, not the exception.

There is an alternative to raising angry children. Ephesians 6:4b instructs, "but bring them up in the nurture and admonition of the Lord" (KJV). A smiliar word "nourish" is also used in 5:29 in reference to how a man treats his body. In that context it is understood that to nourish the body one must include such things as a proper diet, medical care, spiritual development, physical exercise, and sufficient sleep. In other words, a man knows and does what is necessary to take good care of himself.

How well are African American men nourishing their bodies? There is sufficient evidence to suggest that they are not doing well:

(1) Black men are dying from cancer more than ever before, specifically lung cancer. Lung cancer is one of the most preventable cancers around yet our men are dying from it. The prevention is simple—do not smoke.

(2) More African American men than ever before are alcoholics. They refuse to get help. They feel they do not need any help.

(3) African American men are killing themselves at an alarming rate today. Suicide among African American men is growing.

To the extent that to nurture means to care for one's self well and holistically, African American men are not doing well. A man will do no more to nurture others than he will do for himself. It can be concluded therefore, that when it comes to nurturing children African American men have a real problem. The problem is bringing the child up in the nurture and admonition of the Lord when he does less than that for himself.

When it comes to bringing up children in the admonition of the Lord, there is a spiritual deficit in the environment of many homes which is ultimately reflected in our children. In Proverbs 4:3, Solomon says that in his home the environment was such that he felt like a son to his father, King David. David fought more wars, confiscated more land, and expanded the boundaries of the nation of Israel more than any other king. Yet while doing all of this and managing the affairs of the kingdom of Israel, David took the time to make his son feel like a son.

The reason David made his son feel like a son is because he treated him well. Their relationship was one in which the father was proud of the son. David esteemed his son, and he treated him with compassion. Solomon was not at odds with his father. Instead, they had the kind of relationship that caused them to enjoy time together.

It is possible to have a family that has better than adequate shelter, nourishing food, and the best clothing, and yet have a home in which there is a serious spiritual deficit. In such an environment it is not possible to teach children wisdom. This ability to live skillfully, distinguishing between what is really important and what seems to be important, is passed from father to son from heart to heart, not just head to head. The focus is not on being smart but on being wise.

To pass wisdom from heart to heart, there must be a home environment in which hearts are more evident than heads; feelings stronger than attitudes. This is what it means for fathers to bring up their children in the nurture and admonition of the Lord.

The parenting of children in the nurture and admonition of the Lord requires a mother who knows how to mother. Proverbs 4:3b says that Solomon's mother treated him as if he were her only child, "tender and the only son in the sight of my mother." Following in Proverbs 4:4, Solomon says of his father, "He taught me and said to me, 'Let your heart hold fast my words; keep my commandments and live.'" It was the mother who set the environment in the home.

All of the current evidence on parenting in America today supports the conclusion that most of the parenting is done by mothers. However, as I understand Proverbs 4:3b, the children who are best equipped to make wise choices in life are those children who are parented well by their father. Solomon said that his mother set the environment in the home and when the environment was conducive his father taught him. Every son must have a father who teaches him how to carve out for himself a whole life.

In Genesis 22 Abraham offered up his son Isaac in obedience to the command of God. Of the many things that could be said about this story, one stands out. Parents do well to put their children on God's altar and offer them up as an offering to Him to do with as He pleases.

In this situation, God did not ask Abraham for money, time, or talent. God did not ask Abraham for his own life. In this situation God asked Abraham for the life of his son, whom he loved with all his heart.

When Abraham got to the mountain where he was to offer up his son to God, God did not intervene until it was clear that Abraham was going to obey Him and kill his son. When Abraham drew back the knife, an angel of the Lord stepped in and said to Abraham, "Do not stretch out your hand against the lad," and Abraham looked up and saw a ram. The sacrifice had been provided. On their way up the mountain, Isaac asked Abraham where the sacrifice was. Abraham replied "God will provide for Himself the lamb for the burnt offering." And God did provide the offering. Every father needs to know and be able to say to his children, God will provide. . . . and He will.

CHAPTER 22

THE ABUSIVE FATHER AND THE PROVOKED CHILD

O ne of the consequences of a father not managing well the authority the Lord has given him over his children is a child who has been provoked to wrath by his father. Such a child is very angry and often out of control to the point of rebellion.

The issue here is the problem of a child who is rebelling because of the misuse of authority by the father. In order to understand how to manage this type of child, we must first consider the attitude of the father in the context of the home. The father of the child who has been provoked to wrath is a man who:

(1) Rules his home with an iron fist;
(2) Abuses verbally;
(3) Demands obedience;
(4) Lacks satisfaction;
(5) Abuses physically;
(6) Detaches himself emotionally; and
(7) Forgives no one.

Mr. Jones was this kind of father. It was not unusual for him to arouse any one of his children from bed and send that child outside to redo the lawn. He may have determined that it was not done to his satisfaction when he arrived home late. The lateness of the hour did not deter him; he demanded obedience. It was my unfortunate experience to watch each one of Mr. Jones's children grow into seriously rebellious children—failing at everything they attempted to do.

The effect of these attitudes and this kind of behavior perpetrated by a father on a child must be considered in the context of the dependent position of the child. The dependent status of children is such that in reality they have no rights at all because they do not have the authority to make demands. They are totally dependent upon the parents to meet their spiritual, emotional, and physical needs. Thus, in those cases in which a parent for whatever reason refuses to meet the total needs of the child, the child can lose heart and become angry or bitter.

In a home in which conflict, violence and abuse are common, the development of rage in the children is strong. The same is true in divorce. The children of divorced parents are sometimes angry about the divorce.

In dealing with wrath in a child, the parent must first come to anticipate the possibility of wrath developing. It is unrealistic for a parent to think that there will be no residual effect from a poor home environment on the children who grow up in that home. Thus, parents who know that their home has been a place in which there was deprivation, would do well to anticipate wrath in the child. This might also be true of children of single parents. The children of stepparents may have the same problem.

To anticipate the possibility of anger showing up in the child is to be prepared to respond to it when it comes. The response must be one of compassion and understanding. Out of this the parent must move quickly to discover the cause behind the anger in the child. This might necessitate professional counseling. Having discovered the cause, the family must move towards working through the causes to a resolution of the anger.

The child who is angry may express that anger in a variety of ways. He might simply refuse to communicate with his father or other family members. He may become very hostile and express negative aggression towards his father and others in the family. In the case of a girl, she may become sexually active and even deliberately get herself pregnant as an act of rebellion. It is not uncommon for children who are angry to do poorly in school.

The most common response on the part of parents when they have an angry child on their hand is to use corporal punishment. At best this type of punishment might restrain the expression of the anger for a while, but it seldom does anything about the problem itself.

There are several biblical examples of fathers who had children who were angry. The sons of Jacob were angry with Jacob and jealous of Joseph because Joseph received preferential treatment. The other sons of Jacob expressed their anger by selling their brother into slavery and telling their father that he had been killed. David's son, Absalom, was an angry son perhaps provoked by his father's adultery. Absalom expressed his anger by publicly shaming his father by having sex with his concubines and then chasing his father from the throne. Finally, there is the prodigal son who rejected his father's authority and went his way to succumb to decadence.

In these cases, the anger in the child produced rebellion of some kind which ultimately expressed itself in negative aggression. In each case the evidence suggest that the children loved their father, but reacted negatively towards him. In each case the father's response was one of compassion and understanding. Absalom's rebellion, however, cost him his life.

CHAPTER 23

THE BITTER WIFE

The Scriptures are clear in their instructions to the husband about how he is to get along with his wife. To begin with, the husband is to live with his wife in an understanding way, giving her honor as the weaker vessel (1 Pet. 3:7). Then the Scriptures tell the husband not to be bitter against his wife (Col. 3:19). The Bible also instructs the husband to love his wife as Christ loved the church and as he does himself (Eph. 5:25-26). In addition to the instructions to the husband as to how he is to treat his wife, the Scriptures instruct the wife to love her husband (Titus 2:4) and to obey her husband (Eph. 5:22). The word of God is replete with clear instructions to husbands and wives about how they are to live together in harmony.

While the Bible is full of instructions to the family about how they are to live together in harmony, families are often repositories of bitterness which give rise to ongoing conflicts between husbands and wives. When I use the word conflict I mean negative, abusive, and physical expressions on the part of one or both mates towards the other. When I use the word bitter I mean the attitude behind the expressions which are consistently negative and unforgiving.

As I have thought about conflicts between spouses, it seems to me that they come down to two issues. First, there is conflict that arises over the issue of authority in the home. It is a power struggle. Second, there is the conflict that is the result of wrongs suffered and expectations unfulfilled. These two problems are the primary causes behind both bitterness and the conflict that grows out of that bitterness between husbands and wives.

The question then becomes, how does one manage such a situation? Wherever there is conflict the need for compassion and understanding is also present. In managing the conflict that exists between husbands and wives due to the wife's bitterness toward her husband, there must be an attitude of compassion on the husband's part towards his wife. Compassion in this context will not necessarily determine the content of the husbands response, but it will determine his spirit, and set the atmosphere in which the response is given. For a number of husbands there is a lack of compassion on their part towards their wife. Their response to them is couched in a negative and sometimes abusive spirit.

Sue was a faithful church member serving wherever she could. She was not generally a negative person, except when it came to marriage. Whenever the subject of marriage came up, Sue would turn bitter. In many years of listening to Sue talk about marriage I never heard her say more than a few positive words about it. Why was Sue so bitter towards marriage in general and her husband in particular? It turned out that Jack was not the man that Sue thought he was, and she never forgave him for that.

I have found that husbands and wives are often embittered in time because the mate is not who they expected them to be. Dealing with this kind of bitterness means rebuilding the very foundation of the marriage.

The second thing that is necessary in dealing with conflict with the wife is understanding. Understanding has to do with the response which is based upon the cause of the conflict. While it is true that there is a certain amount of conflict in every marriage, it is dangerous to conclude that conflict is part of being married. In other words, conflict is not synonymous with being married. It must be understood that persistent conflict in any marriage will kill the unity, love, and future of that marriage. It is conflict that gives rise to bitterness which is the fruit of an unforgiving spirit.

Persistent conflict can rob the marriage of its intimacy. Many couples complain about the absence of intimacy and sexual satisfaction in their marriage. In more than a few cases the problem is persistent conflict between the couple. The absence of intimacy and sexual satisfaction over an extended period of time gives rise to bitterness. Sexual satisfaction in a marriage contributes to the wife is assurance of her husband's love for her.

To manage conflict, it is necessary for the couple to be committed to the same goals and objectives. This requires the merger of the world of the husband and the world of the wife into one new world that reflects the goals and objectives of both parties.

CHAPTER 24

INSUFFICIENT FINANCES

onflict in the home is an uncomfortable idea, but it is still all too often a reality. The problem most often is not the conflict itself, but the couple's inability to manage it. Either they do not understand the cause behind the conflict or are not equipped to handle it.

One of the problems that contributes to the development of conflict is money. The conflict over money is not, in many instances, a matter of not having enough money, but a matter of who will manage the household finances. This is often combined with poor management of the family resources and the absence of contentment with material possessions. There are instances, however, in which the problem is a lack of money and I will speak to that problem directly.

The issue of poor money management is rooted in the absence of clearly established financial goals to which both the husband and the wife agree. These goals should be reflective of a biblically-based view of money.

In the Christian community the biblical idea of headship is understood by most men to mean that they are automatically in charge of the household finances. The problem is that in many instances the husband has no vision for himself or his family. The fact is, he has never learned how to manage a budget.

The inability to envision long-term family goals and

a deficiency in budgetary management thwart the African American man's success in handling finances. These shortcomings may be attributed to the disparity in higher education between males and females.

In developing a biblically based attitude towards money, there must first be a clear distinction made between the concept of godliness (living the Christian life) and gain. To live godly does not equal financial gain. In this context the point is not how much money or how little money one has. It does not even mean who is in charge of the money management. Rather the attitude of the couple towards money is the issue. The couple must approach life from the perspective that godliness in its substance is itself gain or profit, but it is only so when accompanied by contentment. Contentment means knowing and feeling that one's sufficiency is rooted in Jesus Christ, not money

In the family, God must always be relied upon as the all-sufficient provider so that the couple consistently feels sufficient no matter what the circumstances. Developing a biblically based attitude towards money means not being motivated by greed in one's lifestyle and attitude. To this end, the couple needs to learn how to be happy whether in the midst of plenty or on the fringes of indigence.

This will require of the couple that they learn the lesson of contentment. This lesson is that Christians have a divinely bestowed sufficiency in Christ no matter what their financial or social situation. It is necessary for the couple to be placed in the kind of life situations that will allow them to experience both abundance and want. They must experience God's providential care in order to learn the lesson of contentment.

Couples often find themselves caught in conflict over money. This occurs not because they earn insufficient wages, but because they have allowed themselves to be drawn into competition with the material success of others. The idea of avoiding competition with others brings to mind the necessity of choosing wisely as a couple the lifestyle to which you will aspire. Inherent in the choice of lifestyle is the couple's attitude towards money and possessions. When it comes to lifestyle the bottom line for the Christian is modesty.

In our culture the desire for riches is perhaps the driving force in the marketplace and in the church. This pursuit of material possessions is the seed of greed in people's hearts and greed gives rise to conflict over money—even among Christians.

The late E. Franklin Frazier in his book, *The Black Bourgeoisie* referred to this spirit of materialism among African Americans as conspicuous consumption. Contemporary sociologists refer to African Americans as habitual consumers—not producers. In many instances when it comes to purchasing goods or obtaining services, African Americans are more interested in the cost per month rather than in the total cost over an extended period of time. Such attitudes causes money to be a major source of conflict in the family.

At the bottom of the financial problems of a number of couples is a non-Christian view of money or I should say a carnal view of money. The desire to get rich is a motivation that places emphasis on the desire rather than on what is desired. It is that desire that drives the person to ruin regardless of whether or not they ever become rich.

Overcoming the lust for riches entails developing a wholesome attitude towards money and maintaining that attitude. To this end the couple must constantly eschew the pursuit of riches. Then they must pursue righteousness and fight to keep themselves from falling into the world's trap of materialism. Frazier said that the desire for material things causes the African American child to value money more than careers that benefit mankind. How the money is acquired is inconsequential to them.

It seems clear that such is the case today. Few young adults are interested in jobs through which they can contribute to society. Rather they are interested in those jobs that yield the most money.

Betty and I are entering our thirty-fifth year of marriage. We have three living children, two of whom are adults. We have been in Christian service most of our married life. I was in Bible school, college and then seminary during the first fifteen years of our marriage. During that time, we were also having babies and trying to raise a family. Complicating the situation I developed colitis, a chronic disease,which kept me in and out of the hospital, and at the time I did not have health insurance.

It is difficult to imagine anyone experiencing a level of poverty that was greater than ours. We had no food; the children needed clothing; and the house needed new flooring. In addition to this, I was constantly in need of medical prescriptions.

It was indeed for us "the worst of times and the best of times." The worst was obvious: poverty. The best was the opportunity our circumstances afforded us to depend on the Lord and learn to be content.

There were many nights that I lay silently in bed beside my wife—pretending to be asleep—aching as she cried herself to sleep. We struggled—I endured pain; the children went without; my wife wore panty hose with runs. In spite of all these hardships, she never once threatened to leave.

CHAPTER 25

UNFULFILLED
SEXUAL DESIRES

S exual satisfaction is a natural assumption of most couples as they enter into the bond of matrimony. However, to the surprise of more than a few couples, this "given" is far removed from reality. There are many causes behind the problem of sexual unfulfillment including such things as misunderstanding what sex means to the other, premarital sexual experiences, sexual abuse in the past, rape, impotence in the man, the negative effect of contraceptives, negative sexual attitudes, low self-esteem, poor heath and a host of others.

Let me begin with what sex means to a woman and what sex means to a man. Timothy and Beverly LaHaye, authors of *The Act of Marriage*, have made some interesting observations concerning what sex means to the female and the male.

What sex means to a woman:

- It affirms her womanhood by exalting her self-esteem and confidence.
- It makes her feel desirable to her husband.
- She experiences companionship.
- She experiences his compassion for her.
- She experiences romantic love.
- She experiences affection.
- She experiences his passionate love.
- It satisfies her sex drive.

- It reduces the tension in her body.
- It gives her the ultimate experience of pleasure.

What sex means to a man:

- It satisfies his sex drive.
- It affirms his manhood.
- It enhances his feelings for his wife in a positive way.
- It contributes positively to the environment in the home by reducing the friction in the home caused by unexpressed sexual desires.
- It is his ultimate expression of pleasure.

Just as couples engage in honest and open discussions on other important issues, it is also important that they have discussions about what sex means to each of them. Such a discussion should include means by which they can best work towards meeting each other's needs.

Premarital sexual experience scan lead to several problems which negatively affect sexual fulfillment. Premarital sex can cause: (1) misplaced sexual expectations of the present mate (previous sexual experiences can cause one to have sexual habits and expectations that are not related to their mate); (2) sexual ghosts in the bedroom (premarital sex can cause a mate to try to perform like a previous lover supposedly performed); (3) serious mistrust of the mate's faithfulness; (4) guilt that emanates from having had previous sex partners.

Sexual abuse and rape can leave serious mental scars on their victims. Sexual abuse means experiencing sexual intercourse as a child/teenager at the hands of an older person. This experience can contribute to the inability to experience sexual fulfillment because of the negative experience of sexual abuse. It often prevents the abused mate from entering into the sexual experience with a positive attitude. Rape is an act of violence; it, like sexual abuse, can permanently damage the victim's attitude towards sex in particular and men in general.

Impotence is the inability of a man to have an erection or the inability to maintain an erection. This inability in most instances will negate the couple's sexual activity thereby leaving their desires unfulfilled. Impotence does not mean the absence of sexual desire; it means the inability to perform sexually using the male organ.

Sexual fantasies are sexual illusions. A certain amount of sexual fantasy is a healthy thing; however, the kind of fantasy that craves unattainable performance or imaginary lovers is not good. Sexual fantasies in marriage ought to grow out of a healthy romance rather than stimulation via pornography.

The lack of sexual gratification in marriage exists. How does one manage unfulfilled sexual desires? To begin with, sex therapy is an option if the problem cannot be resolved in other ways. Should the couple choose sex therapy, they should be very prayerful about the counselor's philosophy before becoming clients.

The alternative to professional counseling is agreeing to work together on the problem with the objective of developing a strategy of managing the problem. I use the word manage rather than resolve because in some cases resolution is not possible. Management is through the grace of God. When sex problems become evident, consider the following steps in trying to revitalize your sex life:

(1) Agree that there is more to making love than sexual intercourse. Playing, talking, touching, kissing, lovingly gazing, smelling, listening, cuddling, snuggling, and hugging are part of loving.

(2) Express, in a positive way, at an appropriate time that your needs are not being met. It is very important that both husband and wife know and understand what each desire as it relates to frequency (how often), time preference (when), location (where), pre-activity (foreplay), post-activity (cuddling, snoozing), methods (positions), and sensual enhancement (music, rain, fragrances, candles). When needs are not met, silence is not golden—it is deadly!

(3) Strive together to identify exactly what you think is missing in your sex life. Be specific, not vague.

(4) Be willing to accept responsibility for your part of the problem. In working out a strategy in this area, it is necessary to avoid being defensive. Strive to be transparent and sincere.

(5) Agree together to work towards a positive management strategy that will lead to a healthy satisfying love life. This may mean learning to live with the problem.

(6) Be willing to settle for less for the sake of unity and happiness in the marriage. A decision not to include some things in life may be necessary due to limitations that cannot be altered.

(7) Expand if necessary your definition of sex and sexuality. This means placing emphasis on love-making instead of sex. It means placing as much a premium on what happens in the living room, dining room, bathroom, and kitchen as on what happens in the bedroom.

(8) Make your sex life a matter of persistent prayer and open positive communication. Problems with sex may demand a season of prayer before attempting the act. Thus the couple may want to spend time together in prayer together before engaging in intercourse.

In terms of management in the area of unfulfilled sexual desires, it should be understood that a high priority must be put on self-discipline and self-control. Failure to do so results in unhealthy sexual fantasies. In addition, such a strategy must include the ability to participate in the management of the mate's sexual needs. A well-balanced diet, consistent physical fitness program, and wholesome entertainment should not be overlooked.

PART 5

SEX EDUCATION

CHAPTER 26

SEX EDUCATION
IN THE HOME

Sex education in the home begins with the parent or parents having a positive balanced attitude towards the whole area of sex and sexuality. It is to be understood from the very outset that children tend to mirror the sexual attitudes held by their parents. For more than a few parents this means that the child/children will have no positive education at all from them.

In preparation for this chapter, I asked a sampling of young adults where they learned about sex and sexuality. All of them said that their knowledge came either from the streets, books, movies, or their friends. Not one person said that they were taught at home or at school.

Sex education in the home for girls is too often the emphatic imperative: "Don't do it!" For boys, the warning: "Don't get her pregnant!" The most basic biological functions are cloaked in secrecy and euphemisms, and are left to be discovered by the often bewildered adolescent. Mothers fail to prepare their daughters for their monthly period. Fathers never mention nocturnal emissions (wet dreams) to their sons. Neither would dare admit that masturbation happens among boys and girls.

Ideally, sex education should be taught in the home where the primary teachers are the parents. Parents that want to raise children into adults with a healthy biblically-based attitude towards sex must have such an attitude themselves. This requires more than keeping pornography out of the home; it requires demonstrating positive attitudes towards sex. Parents should not be ashamed. Rather they should show an appreciation for their body in its totality. In addition, sex should be viewed as normal and healthy—and as a gift from a good and loving Father.

Parents must take the initiative to introduce their children to their reproductive organs, making sure that each part is referred to by its anatomical name. This means that penis and vagina are as commonly used as hand. Children should not be allowed to refer to their sex organs by the names that are used in the streets. Boys who see their father in the nude and girls who see their mother in the nude will soon begin to observe that they have the same body parts as that parent. This will lead to questions which will give the parent an opportunity to teach. During such times, the parent should be careful not to answer more than the child is asking.

In order to diminish curiosity, it is helpful to introduce children to the physical anatomy of the opposite sex. Many of the negative sexual attitudes are due to the fact that boys and girls know little to nothing about their opposite's anatomy. This can be done via pictures, books, filmstrips, videos, and anatomically correct models.

Just as children are introduced to their own body and the body of the opposite sex, it is of equal importance for the parent to introduce children to the individual who lives in the body. This addresses the way boys and girls are socialized to relate to each other. It is not unusual to find in both men and women today an attitude which views the other as a sex object. This means that a man's attitude towards a woman is that she is just a "piece of stuff" and the woman views the man as just a "pair of shorts".

Introducing children to the individual who lives in the body means developing in the child a high appreciation for themselves, as opposed to simply focusing on the body. To accomplish this goal, the parent must teach by both words and example that the heart of a person is of utmost importance. It is a more accurate determinant of character than is physical appearance. This means developing in the child the ability to communicate positively with words, emotions, and body language.

It is at this point that biblical convictions about sexual behavior should become a more integral part of the family discussion. The child who develops an attitude toward the opposite sex that focuses only on the body in general and the sex organs in particular, will demonstrate little concern for the individual who lives in that body. Men, in particular, will do a lot of things to a woman's body that they would not do if they had concern for the woman who lives in that body.

By the time children reach adolescence they should have a working knowledge of who they are and a positive appreciation for their body. To the extent that this is so, the adolescent years will be less turbulent and confusing.

The Bible says that each Christian must know how to possess his own body in sanctification and honor, not in lustful passions. At this stage of development the child should have been equipped with sufficient knowledge about sexuality. This is a prerequisite for the management training stage which rapidly follows.

In adolescence the child's body begins to "talk to it" and "tell it" all manner of things about itself. These hormonal utterances manifest themselves in nocturnal emissions, sexual fantasies, giddiness, daydreaming, infatuations, and moodiness. At this point the child most likely will not vocalize these new feelings. The parent must be cognizant of the fact that the child is having such feelings. The role of the parent changes at this point from that of instructor to that of coach or supervisor. This means always being on guard, protecting the child from the detrimental extremes of these feelings which in no small portion are sexual.

At this stage the boy is probably having wet dreams and therefore needs his privacy. The girl is most likely having her period and demands privacy. Both are experiencing sexual desires and must have prudent supervision by the parents. In this stage the parents supervise whatever it is that they have put into their adolescents. Simultaneously they must teach the youth how to manage themselves with these new feelings. It is at this point that spiritual convictions manifest themselves in a real sense. These convictions must ultimately prove strong enough to hold the budding adult to a Christian course of action in the area of his/her own sex and sexuality.

All master teachers know that students should be

taught in an environment conducive to learning. They also know that one of the crucial steps in teaching is demonstration. The Christian home should be the perfect loving environment to teach sex education. Parents should express and demonstrate their affection for one another. Touching, kissing, hugging, playing, and sweet talking are concrete examples of love that youth need to see. Parents should not conceal from their children that, in addition to being mom and dad, they are lovers. All, of course, must be done with discretion and good taste. To avoid being caught in the sexual act, parents should lock their bedroom door. Privacy should be maintained.

Sex education must include a discussion about what sex means to a woman and what sex means to a to man. It has a diversely different import to women than men. Timothy and Beverly LaHaye outline these in their book, *The Act of Marriage.*

A casual analysis of what sex means to men and women will give any parent a clear understanding as to why sex education is important. It is a fact that boys and girls are physically capable of engaging in sex long before they are emotionally or spiritually equipped to handle the experience. Therefore, parents must strive to equip their children with a knowledge of their sexual being and instill convictions that are strong enough to manage that being.

CHAPTER 27

AIDS EDUCATION
IN THE HOME

B ecause AIDS is an important social and medical issue, it demands discussion in the Christian community. AIDS is an acronym for Acquired Immune Deficiency Syndrome. This syndrome is caused by a foreign virus called I-HIV which breaks down the human immune system. When the immune system of the human body fails, the body is unable to fight off diseases and infections that attack it. Without the ability to fight, the body dies. AIDS is a subtle virus in that it is possible to contract the virus and have it lay dormant for years before it begins to affect the body. AIDS is a deadly disease because it robs the body of its ability to recover from any disease. Because there is no known cure, many will die.

It is estimated that there are about one million people in America who have this deadly virus. Hundreds of thousands have already died from the disease. The disease is spreading fastest among people of color in America, most commonly, by sharing contaminated hypodermic needles.

There is much discussion today about the physical and geographical origins of AIDS. Many theories have been suggested, but a definitive origin is yet to be determined. According to some reports, the initial biological outbreak of the disease in this country was among the male homosexual community. The largest community of gay males was in San Francisco. The largest number of

AIDS victims was also in that community. These were primarily young, gay, white males. For a while, AIDS was thought to be a deadly disease confined to the gay community, but this is no longer the case.

Regardless of its origins, the fact is that AIDS is here and in epidemic proportions. It is now being suggested by some that in the not-too-distant future most, if not every, families in America will be affected by this deadly virus. This dire possibility is quite real; the reasons are succinct:

(1) The primary means of transmitting the virus is through the exchange of body fluids such as blood and semen. Not all condoms protect against the transmission of this disease.

(2) The homosexual community is a primary carrier and transmitter of the disease. Homosexuality is a growing alternative lifestyle among males.

(3) Many homosexual men have heterosexual relationships which provides the bridge for the disease to be spread into the heterosexual population.

(4) Intravenous drug users are primary carriers and transmitters of the virus because they share contaminated needles.

(5) An increasing number of babies are born with the virus.

(6) Sexual freedom allows for behavioral practices that are conducive to the rapid spread of the disease. The more partners, the higher the chance of contracting the disease.

(7) Youths are sexually active today with little thought to the idea of safe sex. Thus, untold numbers may be infected now and will not discover it until they are in their 20s.

(8) The idea of safe sex is just that—an idea. No one knows how effective the preventive measures are apart from total abstinence.

There is little doubt that AIDS will make a lasting impact on the global community—both saved and unsaved—across racial and cultural lines. The question is, how are we, as Christians, going to deal with the problem of AIDS? The first problem we must address is our attitude towards those who have the disease. We must develop an attitude of compassion. This means learning to treat people with

AIDS as human beings. I heard a man with AIDS say that after it became known that he had AIDS nobody touched him for two years. Interestingly, those with AIDS whose families do not abandon them actually live longer with fewer complications.

The second thing we must do is learn as much as we can about the virus and how it is transmitted. This will enable us to manage our own health in a proper way. The issue of morality for the Christian has always been a high priority, but the spread of AIDS places an additional incentive to be moral in the area of sexual activity.

As a parent I realize that the issue of morality is not just a matter of biblical conviction and fellowship with God, but is equally a matter of life and death. Gone are the days when sexual promiscuity was viewed as a harmless romp through fertile fields. The young man or woman who elects to become sexually active outside of marriage may in fact be signing his/her own death warrant. For a growing number of people, moral purity is not a matter of Christian conviction, but a matter of life and death.

AIDS education must be a part of sex education in the home. Children must be taught at an early age what AIDS is, how it is transmitted, and exactly who is at risk. The fact is that AIDS is as much a part of the straight community as it is the gay community. Abstinence from sexual intercourse for the non-drug user is the most effective means of avoiding this virus.

Having ministered to a number of families whose relatives were living with and dying of AIDS, I have concluded that there is hardly any disease that carries a more humiliating stigma. The shame felt by a family whose loved one died of AIDS is tremendous.

The assumption is that all AIDS victims are gay, and this is false. This assumption is a major hindrance to the care most receive from the church. For some reason, homosexuality has become the unpardonable sin in the church. While I clearly speak out against it, as God has in His Word, the church has shamefully acted in an unloving and unforgiving manner to those who struggle with homosexuality. The assumption that all persons with AIDS are gay causes the Christian church to feel justified in discriminating against this group of people, when in fact, the church is exactly the place these people need to be.

I remember the day Jack walked into my office, sat down, and with a solemn look said to me, "Pastor Lane, I have AIDS." For a moment we both just sat there staring at each other. Flashing through my mind was the question, how is it possible for Jack to have AIDS since he is obviously not gay? Was Jack gay and the virus was forcing him out of the closet?

It turned out that Jack was not gay; his was a case of bisexual activity. Over the next few months, Jack and I spent many hours together talking about a variety of issues. For a while it seemed that Jack was not even sick. In fact, he was the picture of health—a big, tall, strong man who resembled a professional athlete.

Suddenly, Jack's health took a radical turn for the worse and what had been our secret was a secret no longer. Jack told his wife and they both told their parents that Jack had AIDS. Once the news was out, a strange thing happened: Jack's wife, and both sets of parents never once mentioned the fact that Jack had AIDS. They were in a state of denial. In time Jack's friends began to avoid him. When they could not avoid being in his presence, they avoided touching him. They stood at a safe distance from him out of fear of catching the virus.

In this experience of watching Jack die before he was 30 years old, I came to realize that most persons with AIDS die alone. Often both family and friends neglect or completely abandon them. After Jack's death, it became evident that his widow would be forced to conceal the cause of her husband's death, otherwise she too would be ostracized.

The church must not leave the care for people with AIDS to the unsaved . We must understand that Christians can acquire AIDS as well. The church must develop a heart of compassion for people with AIDS and their families. Christians should remember that 1 Corinthians 6:9-11 says that homosexuality is one of the things from which believers have been saved. It may well be that someone you know was once a homosexual but is now saved. Suppose that believer is HIV positive. Would you care?

PART 6

EQUIPPING FOR THE STRUGGLE

CHAPTER 28

UNDERSTANDING THE STRUGGLE: EPHESIANS 6:10-12

T he African American Christian faces many challenges today that are exciting, challenging, and sometimes intimidating. The church today in many instances seems uncertain about its role in ministering effectively to the Christian family. While the church diligently strives to find its way in its ministry to families, it seems that each individual believer must understand the nature of the spiritual struggle that must be faced on a daily basis.

In studying the Book of Ephesians, I find it interesting that God's instructions to believers regarding developing and maintaining strong and healthy relationships with each other and the family, is sandwiched between the command to be filled with the Spirit (Eph. 5:18) and the exhortation to stand against the powers of evil (6:10).

I gather from this divine arrangement the idea that every believer must understand and appreciate the value of strong relationships in the church and in the home. To develop and maintain such relationships, the Christian must depend on the power of the Holy Spirit in order to develop and maintain a Christian environment in the home. A Christian home is not just for married people. The single Christian is also responsible before God to develop and maintain a Christian environment in their home as are married people. I further conclude from this divine arrangement that the Christian home is the persistent target of the powers of evil.

Christians must understand that the target of the devil and his demons is not the church congregation collectively, but the individual families who make up the membership of the local church. The devil knows that to the extent that he is able to break down and then break up the Christian environment in the home thereby destroying the Christian attitude of family members, he will in time effectively negate the power and influence of the gospel of Jesus Christ.

To understand the nature of the spiritual struggle Christian families face today, a study of Ephesians 6:10-12 may be helpful. The focus of this section of Ephesians is on finishing well in our walk with and service to the Lord. For the Christian there is nothing left to be won. The battle has already been fought between Jesus and Satan. Jesus won that battle once and for all. The task of the believer is not to win anything; all we must do is stand in the victory that Jesus has already won.

The focus in this text is not on a fight or a battle with the powers of evil, but on a struggle between the believer and the powers of evil. We must therefore understand that the whole of the Christian life is a constant struggle between the believer and the devil with his demons.

There is a difference between the spiritual struggle that we have with the devil and the spiritual fight Jesus had with the devil. In the fight that Jesus had with the devil, the goal was to win or prevail over the devil and all the powers of evil once and for all. In our struggle with the devil, the objective is to stand in the victory Christ won in His fight with the devil. We are to stand in spite of the persistent entanglement of our adversary the devil. Let me re-iterate: Jesus and the devil had the spiritual fight. . . . Jesus defeated the devil once and for all. . . . The believer and the devil are in a struggle. . . . Our responsibility is to stand in the victory won by Jesus on Calvary.

In Ephesians 5:18, the command to all believers is to be filled with the Spirit. In this state of being controlled by the Spirit, the believer sings, prays, and submits one to the other, all in ways that are beyond his or her natural attitude and behavior. The filling of the Spirit is all about worship, praise, service, family, and career. It is about living a supernatural lifestyle in the context of everyday life.

In Ephesians 6:10 the command is be strong in the Lord and in the power of His might. The focus here is on how you finish the Christian life given the inevitable lifetime struggle with Satan and his imps. The major challenge for couples is to finish well in life and service to the Lord.

The difference between the filling for the living and the strengthening for the standing is the difference between the power and influence of the flesh (Rom. 7; Gal. 5), and the power and influence of Satan and his imps (Eph. 6:10ff). In the former, the struggle is with one's own internal depravity; with the latter the struggle is with the external forces of evil that are headed by Satan himself. With the former, the believer's victory is based on his/her willingness to yield to the power of the Holy Spirit. With the latter, the believer's victory is based on his/her willingness to do all that is necessary to stand . . . having been dressed themselves in the full armor of God.

Ephesians 6:10 says, "Finally, be strong in the Lord and in the strength of His might." The text could read: Be fortified with power. Compare: Ephesians 3:16, "that He would grant you, according to the riches of His glory, to be strengthened with power through His Spirit in the inner man"; and Colossians 1:11: "strengthened with all power, according to His glorious might, for the attaining of all steadfastness and patience." I take it that these verses are saying that the position one must be in to access the power to stand against the devil is in the Lord. The source of the power with which the believer is to be equipped to stand in his/her struggle with the devil is a power that comes from outside. The source of that power is: "strength of His [God's] might." In the context of our constant struggle with the devil, the power that is necessary to finish well in life and service to our Lord is not a strength that can come from an increase which flows from our internal resources.

Christian couples who finishes well in life and service to the Lord are believers who live the truth expressed in Philippians 4:13, "I can do all things through Him who strengthens me"; "My grace is sufficient for you, for power is perfected in weaknesses; most gladly therefore I would rather boast about my weaknesses, that the power of

Christ may dwell in me" (2 Cor. 12:9). Christians must refuse to embrace the notion that they can make it in life by drawing upon their own natural strength. They should choose rather to acknowledge their weaknesses along with their struggles.

This strength is "in the Lord." It is the "strength of His power." It must be acknowledged that these words have an implied psychological appeal to the human will and calls saved men and women to a sense of personal courage and determination to finish well in their walk with God. It must be noted, however, that the words of the text are "in the Lord and in His strength."

To say that the believer's strength is in the Lord is to say that those who finish well in their service to the Lord must have a strength that is stronger than self discipline. For this struggle is not about a victory to be won but about a peace to be gained and maintained in the context of everyday life circumstances, in spite of the opposition of our adversary the devil.

Having alerted believers to the need for the supernatural strength of the living God to stand in their struggle with evil, the text goes on to inform believers that they are not naturally equipped for this struggle. "Put on the full armor of God, that you may be able to stand against the wiles of the devil" (KJV). The text is saying that the strength believers must have in order to stand in the struggle with the devil is God's strength. We must also note well that the armor that believers must dress themselves in is also God's.

The text says that the substance of the armor in which believers must dress is such that it will be possible to stand and withstand all of the schemes of the devil. You see in order for the armor to protect the saint it must be durable enough to stand up in the struggle no matter how rough the struggle gets. The focus is not on the power that Satan uses to entangle and attempt to put down the believer. No, the focus is on the schemes of the devil. I take it therefore that the emphasis here is on the fact that the power of the devil and his imps are in the schemes they use to cast down the believer.

When I think of the emphasis God places on the need for both divine power and armor in order to stand against the schemes of the devil, I am compelled to conclude that the devil and his imps are master thinkers and strategists. Numerous and varied are their schemes that are designed to defeat the child of God. Thus, the child of God must be equipped to distinguish between that which seems to be important but is not and that which seems to be unimportant and really is important.

You see, Christians, we are no match for the devil at any level. His mind and his experience in defeating and destroying believers are far beyond anything we could possibly survive on our own.

I am a lover of nature. I spend a good deal of time watching films featuring animals in the wild. I have noticed that when a ravenous lion goes hunting, the survival rate of the prey is solely determined by the decision of the targeted animal to remain with or leave its group. The animal that, for whatever reason, is cut off from the group becomes a meal for the predator. So it is with Christians. The devil sets his mind on separating individual saints from the church or group of believers. Once that is accomplished, the believer will most likely fail.

Our struggle is indeed not with flesh and blood. In order to succeed in this spiritual struggle and thus finish well, it is necessary to have a clear understanding of who the enemy is. The enemy of the believer is not other believers, nor is it specifically unsaved people. The struggle is not with flesh and blood.

Some women think that all men are "dogs" and treat them as such. Others tend to think that all an African American man wants from a woman is sex. Some African American men think all women want is someone to take care of them. Then there are those men and women who have bought into the idea that the white man is the great Satan. The nature of the Christian's spiritual struggle is such that it cannot be with flesh and blood, no matter the race, culture or gender.

The meaning of struggle in Ephesians includes much more than the idea contained in the statement "life is a struggle." In this context its intention is to depict hand-to-hand combat in which the enemy will do and use whatever possible to bring down its opponent. Thus, we must understand as Christians that every day we are in a life and death spiritual struggle with the devil. His single goal is to destroy the child of God by any means necessary.

This life and death struggle is not with people, according to the text. This does not mean that the devil does not use people to carry out his schemes. He has no physical body through which to work in this world; therefore, he utilizes the bodies and minds of people. The devil and his demons must use the mouths of people to spew forth their utterances. These evil spirits must employ the legs and bodies of individuals to infiltrate this or that group of believers for the purpose of destroying their unity and testimonies.

The text is saying that Satan uses people to carry forth his schemes. The believer must understand that the person who has evil on his/her agenda is nothing more than a pawn in the hand of Satan and his imps.

In the recent war between Iraq and Kuwait, President George Bush named it "Desert Storm" when America got involved. In that war, Iraq's conflict turned out not to be a struggle with Kuwait but with the world's greatest super power—the United States. Had it been a struggle just with Kuwait, Iraq would have easily won the war. Iraq was, however, no match for America. So it is with believers. If our struggles were just with people who hassle or hurt us, no doubt we could easily win most of those battles. However, when it turns out that our struggle is with the world's second supernatural power it quickly becomes evident that we are no match for such a power.

To be in a struggle with the devil in this day means to be in a struggle with any and every individual, idea, value system and standard that represents the devil and his imps. When a country with whom America is at war captures one of its soldiers, that country treats the captive (though it has no particular hate for that individual) as if he/she is America. The reason this is done is because the country knows full well that the loyalty of that captured soldier is with the country to whom he/she belongs. Thus given a chance that hostage will destroy his captors. So it is with the child of God. We must understand that the loyalty of the unsaved is with his master, the devil. Given the opportunity that person (though in a relationship with a child of God) will bring down the Christian's testimony. Single saints must guard themselves against becoming involved with Satan's pawns.

Our struggle is not with flesh and blood but against the

rulers, against the powers, against the world forces of this darkness, against the spiritual wickedness in the heavenly places. The rulers, the powers, the forces of darkness and the spiritual wickedness in the heavenly places all refer to the kingdom of Satan. In his kingdom there is a vast number of demons of different ranks. There are myriads of ideas, standards and principles that are fitted for doing evil. There are spiritual forces that dominate the atmosphere.

Note the words used to describe that which the believer must struggle against and prevail in order to finish well in their life and ministry, rulers, powers, world forces, spiritual wickedness. Ephesians 6:11b exhorts us to stand against the schemes of the devil. I take it that Satan's schemes against believers are wrapped in this variety of power packages, thrown into the arena and world of the believer and the death struggle is on.

The armor of God is the only equipment that is adequate for such a struggle. Therefore, the believer must put it on to survive the struggle. Again the text in verse 13 says, "Therefore take up the full armor of God [the purpose] . . . that you may be able to resist in the evil day [result] . . . having done everything to stand firm." There is the need in the life of every believer to be equipped with God's power and dressed in God's full armor. The reason believers need such armor is because of who the enemy is. Our struggle is not with flesh and blood.

In the African American community the two weakest institutions are the family and the church. Ironically these are the same institutions that enabled African American people to survive slavery and oppression for more than four hundred years. It is not possible to have a strong church without strong families, nor is it possible to have a strong family without a strong church. Islamic religion is having a rising influence among African American men. Spiritually speaking, the Muslims are doing nothing more than practicing spiritual masturbation. You see, any religion that has no message or song of deliverance is spiritual masturbation. Christianity offers both the message and the song. The risen Christ has the power to transform men into more than well dressed boys.

CHAPTER 29

GETTING FITTED
FOR THE STRUGGLE:
EPHESIANS 6:13

I did not play football or any other major sport as a young man growing up in the small town of Lake Providence, Louisiana. Today as an older man, I am not one who attends many sports activities, although I do watch a good deal of football on television from time to time. Now that I have disqualified myself as one who is qualified to speak authoritatively about football, let me speak for a moment about playing the game of football.

To play the game of football, each player must prepare and dress for the particular position he is playing. Since every football team has both offensive and defensive players, some players prepare mentally and dress to some extent to defend the football by attacking the opposing team. Other players are mentally prepared and dress to some degree, to run the ball with a view to scoring against the opposing team.

In football, the defensive team is not responsible for making scores, though they may occasionally do so; the offensive players do that. The offensive team members are not responsible for preventing the opposing team from scoring, though they may occasionally do so; the defensive team does that. The team that finishes well, by successfully standing and withstanding against the strategies of the opposing team, usually wins the game. Such is the case with football.

In the game of life for the Christian about which I know a great deal, the opposing team is the devil and his demons. Every believer is a player in this game. As a player it is the responsibility of every believer to play both the offensive and the defensive side of the spiritual life. This means being mentally prepared and spiritually equipped for both offensive and defensive moves. The armor that God has provided for the Christian in this life struggle is suited just for such a conflict.

Ephesians 6:13 says, "Therefore take up the full armor of God [the purpose] . . . that you may be able to resist in the evil day [results] . . . having done everything to stand firm." The text is saying that in light of the nature of the Christian's struggle with the supernatural powers of evil, every Christian must be motivated to put forth the effort to take up and put on God's holy armor. Let me put it this way: Having been informed as to who the opposition is in the Christian life—not flesh and blood, but the devil and his demons, and being enlightened, as to the nature of the struggle, which is against the schemes of the devil, Christians must equip themselves with combat armor. This armor belongs to God and is supernatural in substance.

The objective of this armor is for the express purpose of enabling the believer to resist the schemes of the devil in this evil day. In the context of this evil day, every believer must make every effort to accomplish all that is necessary to stand firm. This means that in the Christian's struggle, there is no room for failure. The total objective is to stand and not give an inch.

Before we look at the first three pieces of the armor that the believer is to put on in preparation for standing against the schemes of the devil, let us remind ourselves at this point, that the struggle is against the schemes of the devil. That with which the believer must struggle, and stand, in order to finish well in life and ministry are: rulers, powers, world forces and spiritual wickedness. Ephesians 6:11b tells us to stand against the schemes of the devil. I take it that Satan's schemes against believers are wrapped in these different power packages and thrown into the arena and world of the believer and the death struggle is on.

In a Christian family it is important to realize that all the forces of hell are aligned against you with one objective; namely, that you not finish well in your life and service to the Lord. This evil against which you must stand is not a mere idea, principle, philosophy or standard. This evil is headed by Satan, a real supernatural person.

The first three pieces of armor are truth, righteousness and the gospel of peace. These pieces of the believer's armor are all virtues of the character of believers. Since each believer must individually put on each piece of this armor, even though these virtues are inherent in the salvation experience, the focus here is on the consistent practice of these virtues in the context of every day life.

It is interesting to note that in Ephesians 5:18, the command to be filled with the Spirit is in the passive tense, indicating that it is an experience that results from the believer yielding to the indwelling Holy Spirit. No effort is required on the part of the believer to be filled with the Spirit. In Ephesians 6:13 the command to put on the full armor of God is an aorist imperative, which means that the believer must put forth effort to dress up in God's armor. I should also point out that in both the filling and the dressing, the responsibility of the believer is to obey God's command and do it.

In dressing for this spiritual struggle the first piece of armor handed to the Christian soldier is the belt of truth. Ephesians 6:14 says, "having girded [fastened] your loins with truth." The idea of truth here is not the truth of the gospel by which the believer was saved. In this context, truth refers to the principle of truth, which resulted from believing the gospel and being saved.

This belt of truth is to be fastened around the loins of the believer next to the skin, so that the Christian soldier is able to move about both offensively and defensively in this life and death struggle with Satan and his demons. The belt of truth is honesty, pure motives—no hypocrisy in the believer's life and ministry. It is truth that will not permit deception, and fraud. It is truth that will not allow gossip and deceit. It is the truth that enables the believer to think the best about others until they can no longer do so.

"Take the belt of truth," the text says. It is to be fastened around your loins, so that the schemes of the devil will not be able to catch hold of your life and throw you down by way of a flawed character in the area of truth. Truth is for most Christians a major challenge in terms of relationships.

"Truth" is used four times in the fourth chapter of Ephesians. It is used in 4:15 in the context of Christian fellowship—"speaking the truth in love." Spiritual growth is rooted in the soil of truth. In 4:21 truth is used as that which defines the very essence of Jesus—"just as truth is in Jesus." The foundation of Christian doctrine is truth in Jesus. It is used in 4: 24 as that which characterizes the new self that the believer is to put on after having put off the old self and been renewed in the spirit of the mind. "Put on the new self which in the likeness of God has been created in righteousness and holiness of the truth" It is used in 4: 25 as the expression of the new self in the context of the believer's social life—"Laying aside falsehood, speak truth, each one of you with his neighbor."

It must be noted that the text sets forth truth as that which first and foremost reveals the presence of the new self. "Speak the truth, one with the other." The reason given in 4:25 that obligates believers to speak truth to one another is that we are members of one another. Every man and woman must learn to relate to one another in such a way that it is evident that they recognize their eternal bond one to the other.

The issue of speaking the truth to one another is not merely a matter of deciding to get the facts straight. The real issue in speaking the truth is one of integrity. The issue of integrity is not just about correct information; it is really about the will to be transparent with people.

I find in the Christian community a number of saints who always get the facts straight so that they cannot be accused of lying. However, it is what they choose not to tell you that is the issue. Being truthful means being totally open with people so that they know what you know and think about the situation.

Personal integrity is about being the same in attitude and behavior in private as well as in public. The security belt of the believer is truth in the inner man. In this struggle with the adversary the devil, genuineness is absolutely necessary.

In chapter four the issue for the believer is speaking the truth as an expression of a new life in Christ. In chapter six the focus is on fastening truth about the loins as a means of standing against the schemes of the devil, while continually struggling with those schemes.

In John 8:44, Jesus told the best religious people of His day that they were of their father, the devil, and the works of their father, the devil, they would do. Then Jesus said he (the devil) was a liar from the beginning. In fact he (the devil) is the father of lies, being that he was a liar and a murderer from the beginning.

The whole life of a child of God must be characterized by truth in every relationship and in all ministry. The belt of truth is the believer's heart based on a commitment to genuineness. The belt of truth is the difference between the saint who is nothing more than a "wanna be" and an authentic saint.

Having fastened the belt of truth around the loins, the believer is next handed the breastplate of righteousness. I take it that the belt of truth is designed and worn about the body in such a way that it makes the Christian soldier functional and agile in his/her struggle with the powers of evil. The breastplate of righteousness is designed to cover the vital organs and thus protect them from the weapons of the evil one.

This breastplate is designed to cover both the front and back of the soldier. I am reminded of Proverbs 4:23: "Watch over your heart, for out of it flows the issue of life." I am also reminded of the words of Jesus: "Where your treasure is there will your heart be also." Mark 7 says that it is out of the heart that the mouth speaks. Jeremiah 17:9 says, "The heart is the most deceitful thing there is and desperately wicked. No one can really know how bad it is."

I take it that in living and serving the Lord, being involved as we are in a life and death struggle with the powers of evil in this evil day, we must dress up with the kind of armor that protects our heart.

In considering these verses, note that the heart is inherently inclined towards that which is evil. Thus to stand in this struggle with the devil, the heart must be shielded from the power and influence of the devil. In addition, we must note that the human heart is such that whoever and whatever controls the heart, controls the individual. Thus, the human heart must be protected from its susceptibility to exploitation by the powers of evil.

In this struggle with Satan and the powers of evil, it is not just a matter of being shielded from the assault of the enemy, the heart must be kept from exposing itself to the schemes of the devil. I am saying that the heart of the believer is not altogether loyal to the cause of Christ. Thus it must be protected from the schemes of the devil that will induce it to commit treason against the kingdom of heaven. I have found over the years that many Christians, while extensively involved in Christian service, have come to a time in their lives where their hearts are not in what they are doing in the name of Jesus. Be careful, Christians, that your heart not commit treason against the kingdom of heaven by exposing itself to the schemes of the enemy.

This piece of heart-protecting equipment is called "the breastplate of righteousness." The focus is on the content of this breastplate, namely, righteousness. The breastplate of righteousness is designed to protect the heart from the deceitful schemes of the devil—schemes to which even the saved heart is inherently inclined to accept. I am speaking here of that something inside of you and me that causes us to do evil even though we are trying to do good. (Rom. 7). You see, the flesh is prone to cooperate with the schemes of the devil.

This piece of equipment (the breastplate of righteousness) is not so much about protection from what others can do to you and me, as much as it is about what you and I are inclined to do that which is harmful to our own testimony. In this evil day, pornography, lust, greed, deception, infidelity, etc., are all part and parcel of our culture. These are an integral part of what it means to be American. The devil knows full well that our hearts are already disposed to enjoy any and all of these. Thus, while standing against the schemes of the devil, if we are not careful, we will lose our sensitivity to sin and lose the struggle with the adversary.

The breastplate of righteousness is a heart-level commitment to holiness in one's thinking, attitude and behavior. It's essential to our protection from the evil schemes of the devil who has the appearance of being harmlessly entertaining, but is in fact deadly. This is a character trait; it has to do with the kind of person one is in private as well as in public.

The breastplate of righteousness is the difference between being a Christian who is secular in his/her thinking and behavior, and the kind of Christian who is God-focused. For the secular minded believer, church is nothing more than a social activity; there is no spiritual agenda.

The third piece of equipment is the gospel of peace. It is equipment fitted for the feet. In the Roman army, the soldiers had their feet shod with boots that were suited for their task. They had long cleats in them, fitted the feet well, were durable enough for travel over long distances and over rough ground. Even though the terrain was uneven, these sure-footed soldiers were able to maneuver well and reach their destination.

For the believer the gospel of peace is about two things. First, it is about the gospel that saves the soul. It is that message that is based on and rooted in the death, burial and resurrection of Jesus Christ. It is about simple faith in that message alone for salvation. Second, the gospel of peace is about the effect of that gospel message on the heart of the believer, namely, peace with God combined with the peace of God.

With these two things in mind, I conclude that the believer who has his/her feet shod with the preparation of the gospel, is one who is sure of personal salvation and is confident of God's grace, mercy and protection. This is the kind of Christian who is on his/her way to heaven and knows that. At the same time there is confidence in God's care and provision for them in this life right now.

Such a believer is sure-footed in varied and different circumstances of life, so that, no matter what the situation, he/she is standing on sure doctrinal footing and cannot easily be pushed off-balance.

This is the kind of believer who is able to make peace and serve as an advocate of reconciliation and unity in the church. Satan in his schemes often convinces the believer that he/she is not really saved nor really any different from anyone else. The believer who has on the proper footwear is able to resist this.

Having the feet shod with the preparation of the gospel means being able to always give an answer to anyone who asks you the reason for the hope you have in Christ. It gives one the ability to defend his/her faith in the risen Christ and the written word.

In conclusion, our struggle is not with flesh and blood but with the powers of evil. It is the responsibility of each and every believer to dress up in God's armor so that they will be able to stand individually and collectively. This armor is first and foremost equipment for Christ-like character. It is the kind of equipment that makes one authentic. This is not a struggle for the "wannabe's" but only those who are genuine in their faith and walk with God will qualify.

CHAPTER 30

DRESSING
FOR THE STRUGGLE:
EPHESIANS 6:16

I am told by those who presumably know that the United States military has in its arsenal of artillery a helicopter called the "Cobra." This one piece of equipment is said to possess velocity and firepower capable of completely destroying a professional football stadium within seven seconds. With this kind of weapon aimed in one's direction, it is inconceivable to even think of escaping its destructive powers, much less shielding one's self from its firepower.

In the war with Iraq, the United States used scud missiles that literally decimated whole communities of people along with everything they owned. To be a target of the awesome military technology and firepower of America is to, in fact, be dead.

As I think about the military of our day and how wars are fought , it is clear to me that the individual soldier is hardly significant against the firepower of the opposing country. The military strategists of today target whole communities and countries rather than individuals. In order to kill one person or retaliate against one country, a terrorist bomb may destroy a whole plane full of people .

The weapon on the streets among gangs today is the AK47 with a one-hundred-round clip. I am told that an

AK47 fires about six bullets a second. This means that in less than twenty seconds, this gun can fire one hundred times, killing and wounding hundreds of people. Many drive-by shootings and killings are done with AK47s.

It is my contention that the firepower of the devil and his arsenal of spiritual military might is much like that of the superpowers of our day. The trouble is that the church is equipping God's soldiers with bows and arrows to fight against the contemporary spiritual military arsenal of the Devil.

Current weapons like the Cobra or the scud missile are not biblical examples of what our struggle with the devil is like. To understand the spiritual struggle every believer is involved in, we must look back in history. We must look not at American history, but at Roman history that describes the Roman soldier. History tells us he wore a strong belt around his loins designed and worn to enable him to move with deliberate skill and agility. He also wore a breastplate that covered his back and his chest. This piece of equipment protected the vital organs so that he could survive the battle even if he received a frontal blow or an assault from the back. The soldier's boots had cleats that dug into the soil as they marched from one battle to the other. The cleated boots gave him solid footing as he negotiated terrain that was rough and rocky.

The armor of the Christian soldier is God's armor and the first three pieces of equipment concern Christian character. The belt of truth is the believer's heart-based commitment to authenticity. It is the difference between the church member who is nothing more than a "wannabe" and one who is a genuine saint. The breastplate of righteousness is a heart-level commitment to holiness in thinking, attitude and behavior. This is crucial for protection from the evil schemes of the devil. which, while they may appear harmless, can destroy one's character. The protection we enlist will determine the kind of man or woman we are in private and in public. With the character equipment properly fitted, the Christian soldier is next handed the "shield of faith." "Take up the shield of faith with which you will be able to extinguish all the flaming missiles of the devil," exhorts Ephesians 6:16.

The shield that the Roman soldier carried was two feet wide and four feet long. It was made of wood and covered with rawhide. Before going out to battle the soldier would soak his shield in water so that when ignited arrows were launched by the enemy, the shield would not catch fire and burn, even if the flaming arrow penetrated the shield. The soldier used the shield to protect himself from the arrows of the enemy (both the burning and nonburning ones). If for whatever reason he let his shield down and was struck, he immmediately had three problems. First, he had an arrow in his body and was bleeding; second, his body was on fire; third, his shield was lowered and he was likely to be pierced by additional arrows.

When a soldier was struck and lowered his shield due to the pain from the wound, the soldier next to him was exposed. In battle each soldier's shield was partial protection for the adjacent soldier. Thus when one fell, the one next to him most often was also killed by the enemy.

Ephesians 6:16 says, "In addition to all, [taking up] the shield of faith with which you will be able to extinguish all the flaming missiles of the evil one." This piece of equipment has dual functions. Not only does it have the defensive ability to block flaming missiles, it also has the capability to extinguish them.

The burning arrows represent the temptation of evil: impure thoughts, unloving behavior, false teaching, persecution, doubt, discouragement, despair, just to name a few. All of these flaming arrows are in the hand of the devil and his demons and they are systematically fired at the child of God. The shield of faith in the hand of the believer is to be used to extinguish all such arrows.

It is important at this juncture to look at the word "faith." In Ephesians Paul used the word eight times.

(1) 1:15: "That is why, ever since I heard of your strong *faith* in the Lord Jesus and of the love you have for Christians everywhere" (*Living Bible*). Paul says to the saints at Ephesus that it was the news of their faith in the crucified and risen Christ that caused him to pray for them. It was not news of their church membership or religious involvement that excited Paul; it was their faith in Jesus Christ.

(2) 2:8: "For by grace you have been saved through *faith;* and that not of yourselves, it is the gift of God" (NASB). It is the grace of God through faith that saves from sin.

In other words, faith is the means by which a person is saved.

(3) 3:12: "In whom we have boldness and confident access through *faith* in Him" (NASB). In the Christian life the resources from which the believer gets his/her boldness and confidence by which they access the presence of God is by means of their faith in the risen Lord Jesus.

(4) 3:17: "So that Christ may dwell in your hearts through *faith;* and that you, being rooted and grounded in love" (NASB). It is the believer's heart-based faith in the risen Lord Jesus that roots and grounds him/her in the faith.

(5) 4:5: "One Lord, one *faith*, one baptism"(NASB). Faith is the unifying factor in all of Christianity.

(6) 4:13: "Until we all attain to the unity of the *faith*, and of the knowledge of the Son of God, to a mature man, to the measure of the stature which belongs to the fullness of Christ" (NASB). The goal of discipleship and Christian education is spiritual maturity in which there is unity of faith.

(7) 6:23: "Peace be to the brethren, and love with *faith*, from God the Father and the Lord Jesus Christ" (NASB). Faith and love are the heart and soul of the Christian doctrine.

(8) 6:16: "In addition to all, taking up the shield of *faith* with which you will be able to extinguish all the flaming missiles of the evil one" (NASB). The same faith that caused Paul to pray for the saints at Ephesians, the same faith that saved those to whom Paul wrote at Ephesians, the same faith that equipped the saints to live and walk with God and grow in their spiritual life is said to be the shield that extinguishes all the flaming arrows of the devil.

It is important to know that without faith it is impossible to please God. Without faith it is not possible to stand against the arrows of the devil. The question then must be, just what is this shield of faith that is so functional in our struggle with the devil? It is the ability of the believer to draw upon all the resources that God has provided for him/her to be used at will in the struggle with spiritual forces of wickedness in the heavenly places.

I have said that in preparation for war, the Roman soldier soaked his shield in water so that when it caught a flaming arrow from the enemy, it did not catch fire. The wet wood and the saturated animal skin extinguished the fire of the burning arrow. Christian soldiers must do likewise in preparation for their struggle with the devil. They must soak their shield of faith in the blood of Jesus so that when their faith is struck with the burning arrows of hard times, discouragement and persecution, it will not go up in flames, but will instead extinguish the flames.

The enemy dipped his arrow in oil, set it ablaze and shot it at the target for the express purpose of intimidating and frightening the opposition. Often when the soldiers at whom the burning arrows were fired saw these incoming flaming missiles, they would throw down their shields and run for cover. So it is with Christian soldiers in their struggle with the devil. The arrows that are fired at us by our adversary are designed to scare us so badly that we drop our shield of faith and run for the cover of doubt, depression, and human reasoning.

I have seen many Christian women intimidated by the devil in regard to their single state. They have literally thrown down their faith and sought security in some shallow relationship with a pagan man. Others are frightened into thinking that their biological clock is winding down so they had better grab whomever, get married, and have children. Many are verbally told that their adulthood and womanhood are not validated until they have a ring on their finger . . . to wit—a man! Then there are those single men and women who are pushed to frustration and despair with God because they have not yet succeeded in other personal and professional pursuits. In all of these and many other situations the shield of faith is the only protection the Christian has.

What then is the stuff of which our shield of faith is made? The Christian's shield of faith is made up of the undeniable historical fact that God so loved the world that He gave His only begotten Son that whosoever believes in Him should not perish but shall have everlasting life.

The shield of faith is made up of the truth that Jesus, God's only Son died on the cross, was buried and rose three days later. This shield of faith is covered with the blood of Jesus and the justifying power of the resurrection.

Every saint must know that since God has done all of this for him/her and since He did it all before He was loved by them, surely God will not withhold from them any good thing. The same faith by which this saint was saved must likewise protect him/her from despair during difficult life circumstances. Faith is not only trusting God for what cannot be seen; it is in fact trusting God when there is nothing there to be seen. Our God is a great big God and He can do anything He wants, whenever He wants.

On resurrection morning the disciples of Jesus saw Him and bore witness to the fact that He, Jesus, was alive from the dead. Thomas, one of the twelve disciples somehow was absent when Jesus appeared to the other disciples. When he showed up, the disciples who had seen the resurrected Christ told Thomas that Jesus was alive from the dead. Thomas listened to what they said about Jesus being alive from the dead and then replied, "I do not believe this, and further I will not believe this thing you are saying to me unless and until I see it for myself and put my very own hands into the hole in Jesus' side, the hole I saw the Roman soldier put there. I must also see the nail prints in His hands. Now if I see all of that, then and only then will I be persuaded that Jesus is alive from the dead."

It happened that by the time Thomas finished laying out the condition by which he could be persuaded, Jesus showed up and said to Thomas, "I heard what you said, take your hand and put it into my side and look, here are the nail prints in my hand." When Thomas saw what he needed to see, he said, "Lord ,I believe."

Thomas, in this experience, was getting together his shield of faith. Thomas wanted to be able to say, "I am a witness of the fact that Jesus is alive from the dead." Thomas needed to be able to say something more than, "I heard the other disciples say they saw Him." Thomas needed to be able to say, "I saw Him for myself."

The modern-day saint needs to be able to say for him/herself, I know for myself that Jesus is alive from the dead . . . I know for myself that Jesus lives because He lives in my heart . . . I know for myself that Jesus is alive because He hears and answers my prayers. On Christ the solid rock you must stand; all other ground is sinking sand.

On October 13, 1963, after three years of marriage, my wife Betty gave birth to our first child, a healthy boy. On October 27, 1970, Betty and I buried that first born who suddenly died of heart failure. He was seven years and ten days old when he died. As we stood there staring into the grave as our son was lowered into the ground, I thought How could God do this to me? At the time I was a seminary student and a pastor, but I had no answer to that question.

It is not possible to describe the period of discouragement Betty and I went through during this time. Sometimes it seemed as if my heart would literally explode inside my body. The only thing that kept us going, and I am here to attest to it today, was the undeniable reality that God loved us and had demonstrated that love on Calvary. It was our faith in God that made the difference. We had our shield of faith soaked in the blood of Jesus.

This then is what the church needs today. We need to be able to say, I know for myself that Jesus is alive—risen from the dead. I know for myself that Jesus lives because He lives in my heart. I know for myself that Jesus is alive because He hears and answers my prayers.

CHAPTER 31

DON'T FORGET YOUR HELMET: EPHESIANS 6:17

hen one looks at the helmet of the modern day football player and compares it with the helmet of football players of years past, it is evident that today's game of football is perceived to be far more physical, hard hitting, and even dangerous, than it was in years past. The modern-day football helmet is designed to protect the athletes head and neck from injury due to the the rough and tumble nature of the game.

This new professional football helmet of today is reflective of two things: the kind of injuries sustained in the past and the value of the players. Much has been learned from playing the game of football over the years and the design of today's football helmet reflects this. It's constructed to minimize head and neck injuries unlike those of years past. The new helmet is also a reflection of the high value that the owners place on football players. These athletes have the ability to win games and winning is everything.to the owners,

In the current United States military, the helmet is used more for identification than for protection against the weapons of the enemy. It is virtually impossible for any helmet to protect against the modern day firepower of most opposing armies. Yet each country's military has its

own unique helmet, designed to identify the soldier as belonging to this or that country.

In the Roman army of years past, the soldier was is-
sued each piece of the armor that he was to put on in
preparation for battle. That is, with the exception of the
helmet, each piece was handed to him. When it came to the
helmet, the soldier most often reached down and picked up
his own helmet and placed it on his head. It is important
to note that he took up his helmet before he took up his
sword. No soldier went forth to war without his helmet.
The helmet served as both protection and identification
for the Roman soldier. It protected the soldier from the arrows of the enemy and it identified the soldier as belonging to the Roman army. Couples who determine to finish
well in their life and service to their Lord must have on the
proper head dress.

Ephesians 6:17 says, "take up the helmet of salvation." This is a reference to the believer's identification
with the army of the Lord Jesus. It protects the believer's
head from the fiery missiles/arrows of the enemy. The
helmet of salvation consists of the believer's present deliverance from the power, penalty and ultimately, the very
presence of sin.

In this spiritual struggle with the devil and his
demons, the believer stands in the present experience of
being free from the dominating power, influence, and control of sin over his/her life. In addition, the believer has
settled in his/her mind the reality of the hope of ultimate
deliverance from the presence of sin.

So many saints are trying to stand for Jesus in their
life and service while at the same time they struggle with
the issue of whether or not they are genuinely saved. Having on the proper head gear in this struggle with the forces
of evil means being convinced that you are genuinely
saved. Salvation in this context has to do with victory
over personal human depravity. It has to do with being as-
sured of who you are and to whom you belong.

It is important to say that without the helmet of salvation the believer is in danger of losing the struggle. The
lack of this piece of armor causes uncertainty about who
Jesus is and doctrinal intimidation as to what salvation
really means.

Christians who do not put on their helmet of salva-

DON'T FORGET YOUR HELMET: EPHESIANS 6:17

tion may be saved but they lack assurance of their salvation. They may have been born again but they do not have confidence in the eternality of their salvation.

Having on the helmet of salvation means that when it comes to an inquiry about who Jesus is and what salvation means, the believer is able to give an answer to everyone who asks for a reason of the hope that they have. This hope in Jesus is not based on the saint's spiritual perfection but on a personal relationship with God through Jesus Christ.

The helmet of salvation is not so much about external circumstances affecting the believer as it is about what is settled internally in the mind and spirit of the believer while in the midst of these circumstances.

Much of the struggle with which married Christians must contend in standing against the schemes of the devil is related to the mind and spirit. The struggle is about steadfastness in the faith, mind and heart. It is about understanding what it is that all believers have in Christ Jesus. The helmet of salvation means knowing that every saint has an inheritance in Christ Jesus that cannot be altered by circumstances in this life.

This inheritance to which we have been appointed is said to be "in Him," [Eph. 1:4]. "In Him" refers to the risen Christ. However, we must pay close attention to the fact that there are prerequisites to obtaining this inheritance in Christ. As recorded in Ephesians 1:13 it occurs, "after listening to the message of truth, the gospel of your salvation." The text is saying that in order to gain access to this inheritance, it is necessary to first hear the gospel message. The helmet of salvation is being cognizant of what it is we have as believers in Christ.

The saint who does not wear the helmet of salvation will tend to focus on what it is they do not have in this life, with little focus on life eternal. The helmet of salvation equips the believer to keep a clear head spiritually so that the focus is on his/her relationship with God through Jesus Christ no matter what the circumstances are in life.

To have the helmet of salvation is to have clarity on the "how" of salvation. It is to be fully persuaded that salvation is free to all who will take it. The Bible says, "By grace we have been saved." Salvation by grace means that salvation is a gift from God. It is not possible to contribute anything to our salvation. Thus to say, "I joined the church," or "I grew up in church; therefore, I am saved," is to say that you are not saved. Salvation is a gift from God. By grace you are saved.

It is important to understand that being morally good will not obtain for you a right relationship with God. It is equally important to know that being morally bad will not sentence you to hell. It is true that saved people will live righteously, but not all who live righteously are saved. It is also true that immoral people tend not to be saved; nevertheless, it is what people believe about Jesus that determines their eternal destiny, not the bad or good that they do. Salvation is a gift from God.

The helmet of salvation means having confidence in the eternality of salvation. It is to know beyond a shadow of a doubt that it is not possible to lose your salvation. Christians must not think that every time they fail in their walk with God they need to be saved again.

It is interesting to note that Ephesians 4:30 focuses on the believer grieving the Holy Spirit "And do not grieve the Holy Spirit of God by whom you were sealed for the day of redemption." I think we must pay close attention to these words. Indeed it does teach that believers have been sealed by the Holy spirit for the day of redemption. It is not possible for anything or anybody to break that seal and take away our salvation.

Having put on the helmet of salvation, the soldier picks up his final piece of equipment which is the sword of the Spirit. Ephesians 6:17 exhorts, "Take the sword of the Spirit which is the word of God." The text could read, take the sword that belongs to the Spirit which is the word of God. We must note first and foremost that this sword that the soldier has is the word of God, in addition to belonging to the Holy Spirit.

The Roman soldier used his sword both offensively and defensively in his battle with the enemy. Without his sword the soldier could not stand against the assault of the enemy, nor could he effectively assault the enemy. The use of the sword in a battle meant that the soldier was engaged up close and personal with the enemy. He did not customarily throw his sword at the enemy. The very life of this man depended on his ability to hold on to and effectively use his sword both offensively and defensively.

With this image in mind, I take it that as Christians engaged in this spiritual struggle with the devil, success in standing in the struggle and thus finishing well in this up close and personal struggle with the enemy is dependent upon being proficient in handling the word of God. This means being seriously involved in either being discipled or discipling others.

In Luke 4 we have an example of how our Savior used the Word of God defensively in his struggle with the devil. When the devil came after Jesus with the schemes of pride, natural desire and compromise, Jesus used the sword of the Spirit (the Word of God) to block and cast down these assaults.

The sword of the Spirit is the Word of God, according to the text. I take it that this means that the believer must be fully convinced that the Bible in its entirety is inspired by God. To put it another way, the child of God must know for sure that the Bible was not written and compiled by clever men and women who were determined to express their own opinions and ideas. Rather holy men and women penned the words as they were carried along by the Holy Spirit. The Bible is inspired of God. This means that every word of the Bible came from the mind and heart of the living God. The central agent in communicating the word of God to men and women was the Holy Spirit, thus it is in fact the sword of the Spirit.

In this struggle with the devil, believers must use the word of God to attack the schemes of the devil. Likewise, they must also use the word of God to defend themselves against the schemes of the devil.

The sword of the Spirit, which is the Word of God, is the believer's weapon to be used is this spiritual struggle. Second Corinthians 10:4-5 says, "The weapons of our warfare are not carnal [but spiritual]."

The Bible says that the way a young man keeps his life pure is by obeying the Word of God (Ps. 119:9). The Bible also says, "Thy word I have treasured in my heart that I might not sin against Thee" (v. 11). Therefore, discipleship is an essential ingredient in the process of standing in this struggle with the forces of evil.

IN TOUCH:
EPHESIANS 6:18

In our present day world, it is evident that sports are the "in" thing for most people. It does not really matter whether the players are professional or just amateurs playing for the joy of it. It can almost be said that the athlete of today is revered, envied, emulated . . . idolized.

There is a prevailing attitude among a vast majority of people today that winning at whatever the cost is the goal of any sports activity. In the name of winning, almost anything and everything is sacrificed. A young Olympic hopeful became anorexic trying to maintain the diminutive size she desired. This gymnast, as reported on a news show, weighed 40 pounds the day she died. The professional athlete can be as nasty as he/she wants to be . . . just as long as he/she keeps on winning.

Though I know very little about how the game of football is actually played, I have learned that no matter how good the athlete is, there is a coach who calls the shots. The player, whether an offensive or defensive player, a rookie or a pro, is in constant communication with his immediate coach, who is, in turn, in touch with the head coach. It is not possible to play the game of football and win if the players are not in touch with the head coach.

The same is true of the soldier. No matter how well-equipped the soldier, unless he is in communication with the commander-in-chief, the whole battle can be lost. In any struggle with an enemy, it is not only necessary to understand the nature of the struggle and the enemy, it is also necessary to know who is in charge of the army and to be in constant touch with that person.

It has been my observation that more than a few saints try to live the Christian life in a social and spiritual vacuum—out of touch with reality. Many strive to be holy while being out of touch with the church and the body of believers. Still others think that spouting the right spiritual jargon means that they are in touch with God.

The Christian soldier at this point is fully aware of the nature of the struggle. He knows that the enemy is not flesh and blood but all the powers of evil. The soldier is clear on his/her assignment, namely, to stand against the forces of evil in this evil day. The soldier is fully dressed in all of God's spiritual armor: (1) the belt of truth, (2) the breastplate of righteousness, (3) the boots of the gospel of peace, (4) the shield of faith, (5) the helmet of salvation, and (6) the sword of the Spirit, which is the Word of God.

We must not think that the soldier is fully prepared for the struggle because he/she has on all of the right equipment. Being properly dressed in the armor of God is a prerequisite to engaging in the struggle with the devil and his demons. All of the armor that the soldier has on belongs to God. In addition, everything the soldier of the Lord has on has made him/her dependent on the Lord. Christians must resist the idea that independence is the way to go. The saint who attempts to stand alone in a struggle with the devil and his demons will not stand. The whole of the armor of God is designed to make the believer dependent upon Him . . . creating the absolute necessity of being in constant touch with Him in prayer.

Ephesians 6:18 says, "with all prayer and petition pray at all times in the Spirit." The text is saying that to finish well in our struggle with the powers of evil, the believer must be in constant touch with the living Lord Jesus Christ. The question that must be asked at this point is, are you in touch with Jesus? I am not asking if you are saved or not, nor am I asking if you know who the enemy is. I am not even asking if you are properly dressed for the struggle. My question is, are you in touch with Jesus? Are you constantly talking to the one in whose victory over all the forces of evil you are standing?

Ephesians 6:18 continues, "and with this in view be on the alert with all perseverance and petition for all the saints." When the text says "with this in view" it is referring to the statement "with all prayer and petition pray at all times in the Spirit." Thus the child of God who is to finish well in the spiritual struggle is characterized as one who has an attitude of prayer and a spirit of alertness.

As it pertains to prayer, more than a few Christians are not at all alert. The call from the Lord to the Christian soldier to be alert is reflective of the fact that we are in evil days and seriously engaged in a spiritual struggle with the powers of evil.

Ephesians 5:16 says that we must make the most of every minute because the days are evil. I take it that the call of God today is for all of us (His children) to be on the alert and about the business of standing and shining as His light in this evil day. Sometimes it is necessary for some of God's children to cast their light into an area of darkness that others are not fitted to minister. Each of us must know for ourselves what it is that God has called us to so that we do not spend our time unwisely. The saint who knows what it is that God has called him/her to do and is in touch with the living God in prayer is able to distinguish between that which seems to be important but is not, and that which seems to be important, and really is.

Ephesians 6:18 says, "pray at all times in the Spirit." The text is saying that being in touch with the living God means praying in the power of the Holy Spirit. Consider the role of the Holy Spirit in the life of the child of God as presented in Ephesians:

(1) 1:13—In Him, you also, after listening to the message of truth, the gospel of your salvation—having also believed, you were sealed in Him with the Holy Spirit of promise,

(2) 2:18—for through Him we both have our access in one Spirit to the Father;

(3) 3:16—that He would grant you, according to the riches of His glory, to be strengthened with power through His Spirit in the inner man;

(4) 5:18—And do not get drunk with wine, for that is dissipation, but be filled with the Spirit;

(5) 5:17—And take the helmet of salvation, and the sword of the Spirit, which is the Word of God;

(6) 5:18—With all prayer and petition, pray at all times in the Spirit, and with this in view, be on the alert with all perseverance and petition for all the saints.

Being in touch with the living God means knowing the role of the Holy Spirit in the life and service of the believer. These verses from Ephesians tells us six things about the role of the Holy spirit in our lives:

- We are sealed in Him (Christ) with the Holy Spirit of promise;
- We have access in one Spirit (the Holy Spirit) to the Father;
- We are strengthened with power through His Spirit (the Holy Spirit);
- We are to be filled with the (Holy) Spirit;
- We have the sword of the (Holy) Spirit, which is the Word of God;
- We are to pray at all times in the (Holy) Spirit.

I find it both interesting and instructive that the text says to pray in the Spirit. You see, praying in the Spirit to the living God means talking to God the Father in the name of the Son but through the medium of the Holy Spirit. It is helpful to know that the same Holy Spirit of God that is so involved in our walk with God is the agent through whom we keep in touch with the Father. Praying is a supernatural thing that requires the enabling power of God the Holy Spirit.

We must pay attention to the words *prayer, perseverance,* and *alertness.* These words suggest that in this spiritual battle with the devil and his demons, the believer's ability to persevere and remain constantly alert is dependent upon that believer's prayer life. It is possible to have on all of the right spiritual gear and not be able to stand your ground in this struggle with evil forces. The key to standing is prayer.

One of the most important things I have learned as a pastor is that effective living and ministry are not dependent upon academic credentials. As important as they may be, effective ministry is bound up in the believers availability to and communication with the Lord Jesus Christ. As a Seminary student I learned how to study and do scholarly research. As a husband and a father who is also in ministry I learned to be in touch with the Master.

There are few areas in the life of Christians, and especially preachers, that will prove to be more crucial to their success than the family. Yet for more than a few Christians, the family ranks lowest on their list of priorities. Minimum time, effort, and involvement are devoted to it.

In the world of Christian leadership, many hold the conviction that their priorities in life should be God first, family second, and ministry third. Few people who have worked in vocational ministry have found this rigid order to be functional. The truth is that there are times when anyone of the three could rank first; the order is flexible—not static. Many times my wife and children must have my number one spot in terms of time and energy. At other times the ministry must take center court.

In the six sections of this book, I have sought to make a biblical case for the African American family in the context of this ever-changing society. I may have raised more questions than I answered. I may have offered simplistic answers to complicated questions. Yet I hope I have evidenced the courage God gave me to step up to the table and say something about the family of America's blacks of African descent.

I leave this prophetic word with you: should it be that the church does not begin again to involve itself in the struggle of the African American family as it has in the past, the 21st century may well be as destructive to the African American community as the 20th century was productive. I am sounding the clarion call to African American preachers to get their houses in order and begin again to focus on the family.

NOTES

NOTES

NOTES